A World Apart

The Story of Hebridean Shipping

Andrew Clark

The *Chevalier* (top) and *King George V* (bottom) in Oban Bay

Contents

First published in the United Kingdom, 2010,
by Stenlake Publishing Ltd.
54-58 Mill Square,
Catrine,
KA5 6RD

Telephone: 01290 551122
www.stenlake.co.uk

ISBN 9781840335101

Introduction

Fifty years ago I was lucky enough to visit the Western Isles of Scotland before the advent of car ferries. 'Lucky' in this context is an ambiguous word. Many islanders today regard the pre-car ferry era as best forgotten, a time of low income, inefficient transport links and limited opportunity. The modern era of heavily subsidised ferry services has transformed Hebridean life, multiplying the number of visitors, fuelling investment and making a trip to the mainland a relatively quick, cheap and pleasurable activity. Those things can only be good, because they are in accordance with the increased affordability and opportunity of 21st century life.

But for visitors, the lure of the Hebrides has always been as much about travelling as about arriving. The journey itself may not be the destination, but it is indelibly bound up with it: the easier that journey becomes, the more we take it for granted. The very fact that, half a century ago, the means of travel was often very slow and unpredictable was part of its charm, and part of the wider lure of the Hebridean landscape and its people. It helps to explain why nostalgia for the ships of yesteryear is as strong as interest in today's ultra-functional fleet. Those elegant old ships symbolised a way of life that made the Hebrides a world apart, more individualistic and often bound up with the innocence of youth – a way of life that has been swept away by the hectic demands and high-speed communications of the modern world. Today's fleet of ferries may lack the beauty of yesteryear, but the journeys they make still carry an echo of that past, as anyone who has set sail from Mallaig to the Small Isles on the *Lochnevis* will know, or from Kennacraig to Colonsay on the *Isle of Arran*, or from Oban to Coll on the *Lord of the Isles*.

My love of the Western Isles was kindled between the ages of nine and eighteen when, at my initiative but my parents' expense, I made similar journeys on a previous generation of ships in the 1960s. When you walked from the East Loch Pier at Tarbert, Loch Fyne, across the narrow isthmus to West Loch Tarbert, you could not mistake the difference of atmosphere. You stepped into another world – gentler, quieter, sometimes quite forbidding, somehow more magical. Who could ever forget the sight of the tiny Gigha flit-boat coming alongside the *Lochiel* for a precarious transfer of passengers and mail at the north end of the island? Or the scene on the pier at Castlebay, Barra, at seven in the evening when the *Claymore* tied up after its leisurely voyage across the Minch? Or the midsummer panorama of sun and sea as the *King George V* weighed anchor at Iona for the return sailing to Oban?

Like many who read this book, my attitude to the Western Isles is governed by the fact that I came to them as an outsider, attracted by the magnetism of their scenery, their history, their ecology, their remoteness and easy pace – a magnetism intensified by the sea journey that is necessary to reach them. Those qualities still hold good. Despite the changes of the past half-century, the Hebrides remain environmentally and culturally 'a world apart' from mainland Britain, while being palpably part of a modern transport system. To understand how that system evolved, it is necessary to dip into the past. That is the purpose of this book.

Andrew Clark
Glasgow
June 2010

Acknowledgements

After publishing my book on *Old Millport* in 2005, Richard Stenlake asked me what I would like to do next. This book is the result. I am grateful to him for pointing the way, sourcing many of the illustrations and waiting patiently for the text. Other photographs and postcards were kindly made available by A.E. Bennett, Norman Brown, Stuart Craig, Graeme Dunlop, Susan Forrest, John Goss, Harold Jordan, Willie Macdonald, Fraser MacHaffie, Patrick Maclagan, Ron Murray, Colin Tucker, Caledonian Maritime Assets Ltd, the Newall Dunn Collection and the Scottish Branch of the Paddle Steamer Preservation Society. Graham Langmuir's pictures of the *Claymore* and *Hebrides* at Tobermory, *Iona* at Ullapool, *Lochearn* in Loch Scavaig and *Loch Seaforth* at Armadale are reproduced courtesy of the Mitchell Library, Glasgow; and Tom Duthie's pictures of the *Gondolier* and *Loch Carron* courtesy of the Clyde River Steamer Club. Ian McCrorie's writings on shipping services in the Hebrides have been a source of constant illumination. Louise Boyle, Alex Forrest, Callum Johnston, Iain MacLeod and Eric Schofield have given invaluable help.

In The Beginning

In the summer of 1812 a 13-year old Port Glasgow boy watched with mounting fascination as a boat took shape near his home on the lower banks of the Clyde, the like of which no man had seen. It was the world's first seagoing steamship, and it was named the *Comet*. The boy's name was David Hutcheson. In their separate ways they would both revolutionise sea transport in the West of Scotland, bequeathing a network of services that remains in place to this day.

The *Comet* was the brainchild of Henry Bell, a former mayor of Helensburgh, who developed his revolutionary boat in co-operation with a Glasgow engineer, John Robertson, and a Port Glasgow shipbuilder, John Wood. The ship was launched with all her machinery on board and steam up. Her most novel feature was a set of two paddle-wheels on either side, each with four shovel-like paddles. The engine, producing about three horse-power, was situated aft of a long, slim funnel, which doubled as a mast and supported a sail. She had a small cabin aft of the helmsman, with two flights of steps down each side.

On 5th August 1812 Bell advertised passenger-only sailings in his "handsome Vessel to ply upon the River Clyde between Glasgow and Greenock – to sail with the Power of Wind, Air, and Steam". The *Comet* was to leave Glasgow's Broomielaw on Tuesdays, Thursdays and Saturdays around midday "or at such hour thereafter as may answer from the state of the tide", and to return from Greenock on Mondays, Wednesdays and Fridays. The boat was also to be available for passengers wishing to continue from Greenock to Helensburgh.

The *Comet's* debut came 36 years after the first successful appliance of steam power to a commercial enterprise on land – an advance made possible by the experiments of another Scot, James Watt. She was not the world's first steam-powered boat: that honour falls to various experimental river boats in the United States and Scotland in the 1790s, the latter giving rise to the *Charlotte Dundas*, a short-lived stern-wheeler on the Forth and Clyde Canal.

But as Europe's first commercial steamship, the *Comet* blazed a trail – that of dependable, engine-driven sea transport – that continues 200 years later. On her trial run on 6th August 1812, she took three and a half hours to reach Greenock from Glasgow. It was a huge advance on the 10 to 12 hours taken by fly-boats, until then the customary form of sea transport powered by sail and oar.

The *Comet* was too small to enable Bell to pay off the debts incurred in developing his prototype steamer, and almost overnight he found himself outmanoeuvred by rival operators. Within four years 20 other steamers had been built. Bell lengthened the *Comet*, simplified the paddle mechanism, took her to the Forth and then, after a further lengthening in 1818, put her on a less competitive route – from Glasgow to Fort William via the Crinan Canal, a journey that took four days. The *Comet's* first such voyage took place in September 1820. Three months later she met her end south of Oban, after being hit by a rip-tide and lifted on to the rocks at Craignish Point. No lives were lost but she was a wreck. Only the engine was salvaged.

The *Comet,* a replica of which was built for her 150th anniversary in 1962 (above and opposite page), inaugurated sea transport as we know it today in the Highlands and Islands, powered by mechanical engines rather than by sail and oar in an open boat. By July 1821 Bell had commissioned a bigger, better *Comet* which, after the completion of the Caledonian Canal in 1822, extended her predecessor's voyage from Fort William to Inverness. She also met a tragic end, colliding with another ship in October 1825 with the loss of 62 lives.

By that time five other steamboats were plying in the Western Isles – the *Ben-Nevis, Stirling Castle, Highland Chieftain, Highlander* and *Maid of Islay,* all run by private entrepreneurs and some ranging as far as Tobermory, Iona and Portree. In the late 1820s the *Ben-Nevis* became the first steamboat to venture regularly across the Minch to Stornoway, but the honour of being the first genuinely Hebridean steamer falls to the *Maid of Islay*: unlike the others, which journeyed from the Clyde, she originated her sailings north of the Kintyre Peninsula. Based at Portree, she left on Mondays for Tobermory, Oban and West Loch Tarbert, inaugurating a connection there with steamers bringing passengers from Glasgow to Tarbert on Loch Fyne. On Wednesdays she sailed to Iona and Staffa, before heading back to Portree at the end of the week.

Thanks to the growing size, number and sophistication of steamships in the 1830s, new tonnage became too long to fit the locks of the Crinan Canal, and so began the era of steamer sailings round the Mull of Kintyre. But the canal continued to act as an important artery – especially after the introduction of a track-boat in 1838, which reduced the need for Clyde-based steamers to continue northwards. Thereafter passengers for the Highlands transferred to a canal boat at Ardrishaig and continued by sea-going steamboat at Crinan. In the 1840s iron-built ships began to replace their wooden predecessors. The same period saw a consolidation of the various shipping interests in the Highlands and Islands to the point where, by 1850, one firm, owned by the Glasgow-born brothers George and James Burns, had established itself as the dominant operator.

This is where David Hutcheson, who had witnessed the launch of the *Comet* in 1812, comes back into the story, for he was manager of the Burns brothers' West Highland interests. He had left Port Glasgow in 1817 to work as a shipping clerk in Glasgow – the start of a career that would make him the pivotal figure in the improvement of shipping services in the Western Isles.

In the 1830s and 1840s the shipping empire of G. & J. Burns grew to the point where they controlled the trade from Glasgow to Liverpool and Ireland. They also became founding partners with Samuel Cunard in the first steamship company to operate a mail service across the Atlantic.

In this context G. & J. Burns' Clyde and West Highland interests were of decreasing importance. In 1851 they divested themselves of that part of their business, handing their Clyde river boats to Denny, the Dumbarton shipbuilder, who quickly resold them, and their West Highland interests (including the Glasgow-Ardrishaig service but not the Loch Fyne cargo trade) to David Hutcheson and his younger brother Alexander. A condition of sale was that the Hutchesons' new company should have a third partner – the Burns brothers' nephew David MacBrayne, whose name remains the symbol of Hebridean shipping services to this day.

David Hutcheson, the senior partner, was a popular figure throughout the West of Scotland: there is a memorial on the island of Kerrera, visible to anyone leaving Oban Bay by ship, "erected by a grateful public in memory of David Hutcheson, by whose energy and enterprise the benefits of greatly improved steam communication were conferred on the West Highlands and Islands of Scotland."

At the outset Hutcheson's company owned eight steamers. The *Pioneer* (below at Iona and below opposite at Tobermory, both late in her career) operated the Glasgow-Ardrishaig service. The *Shandon*, the first Hebridean steamer to bear the red-with-black-top funnel colouring that remains such a distinctive part of the scenery, operated the Crinan-Oban-Corpach run, connecting with the *Edinburgh Castle* on the Caledonian Canal and thereafter the *Curlew* on the Moray Firth. The *Duntroon Castle* sailed from Glasgow round the Mull of Kintyre to Portree, while the *Cygnet* and *Lapwing* operated the all-the-way Inverness service via the Crinan Canal. The *Dolphin* sailed from Oban to Staffa, Iona and Glencoe, and there were two Crinan Canal track-boats, the *Maid of Perth* and *Sunbeam*.

Over the following 25 years, until Hutcheson's retirement in 1876, his company expanded beyond recognition. In the late 1850s it established a year-round Stornoway service and took over the Loch Fyne cargo run. Starting with the 1852 *Mountaineer* (below, stranded off Lismore), a succession of splendid new ships joined the fleet, resulting in higher standards of comfort and service. By the time David MacBrayne (right) became sole proprietor in 1878, the business was a highly profitable one, taking advantage of Victorian tourists' wish to explore the islands' unspoilt beauty and of islanders' desire to sell their grain, cattle hides and fish at mainland markets. In little more than half a century, the Hebrides had developed from being a remote outcrop of the British Isles, accessible only by open boat, to being part of a safe, reliable transport system.

This is one of the earliest photographs of a ship built for service in the Western Isles. It shows the *Mary Jane* in the spring of 1858 at Tarbert, Loch Fyne – not at the 'Columba Pier' outside the town where steamers have traditionally berthed for a century and more, but the original pier in the inner harbour where a modern fishing wharf now stands. Built in 1846 for James Matheson of Stornoway, a private shipowner who named her after his wife, the *Mary Jane* was initially placed on a service from Glasgow to Skye and Lewis. She had a typical mid 19th century paddle steamer design – flush-decked (no deck houses), with funnel abaft the paddle-boxes – but with the distinctive fiddle-bow and bowsprit that was to grace several of her West Highland successors. She joined the Hutcheson fleet in 1857, sailing on the Glasgow-Loch Fyne run until 1875, when she was given an extensive refit and a new name. As the *Glencoe*, she was to become one of the best known, most versatile and longest-serving ships ever to grace Hebridean waters.

The *Glencoe* emerged from her 1875 refit with a slanting bow, a deck-saloon aft and only one mast: less elegant, maybe, but more comfortable. Over the following 55 years she served on most of the Hutcheson/MacBrayne routes, including the Ardrishaig and Loch Goil mail services on the Clyde, and the Islay and Portree runs in the Hebrides. She is pictured at Armadale, Skye, in the 1920s.

The *Glencoe* was finally withdrawn in May 1931. The following month, before heading for the breaker's yard at Ardrossan, she spent Glasgow Civic Week at the Broomielaw, berthed alongside the newest member of the MacBrayne fleet, the diesel-electric motor vessel *Lochfyne*. The juxtaposition of old and new was designed to show how far ship design had come in the 85 years since the commissioning of the *Glencoe*, which was described in the Glasgow press as "this most interesting survivor of bygone days".

The *Inverary Castle* at the Old Pier, Tarbert, in the late 1870s. Cattle-loading was a common sight on the shores of Loch Fyne for much of the 19th century, and it often involved the *Inverary Castle*, which spent most of her working life on the cargo run to the town whose name she bore. Leaving Glasgow three days a week at 6am, she would make leisurely progress down-river, through the Kyles of Bute and up Loch Fyne, calling at numerous intermediate ports before reaching her destination in the evening. Built in 1839, the *Inverary Castle* was owned by a variety of shipping interests before passing into the hands of David Hutcheson & Co in 1857. Occasionally she would be called upon to deputise in West Highland waters, such as on a cargo run to Oban in 1859 while the Crinan Canal was closed, Glasgow-Inverness in April 1862 and Glasgow-Islay in January 1863. She was lengthened in 1862 and 1873, fitted with feathering floats in 1868 and later had a deck saloon added near the stern. The spelling of her name was changed to *Inveraray Castle* in 1874. By that time she was established as MacBrayne's oldest steamer, a distinction she held until her withdrawal in 1892.

Left: The *Islay*, first of three 19th century ships to bear the name, is pictured in the dry dock of Tod & McGregor at Meadowside (the Clyde shipyard where the *Inverary Castle* and *Mary Jane* had also been built). Owned by Walter Frederick Campbell, she was one of the first steamers to be made of iron, entering service in 1849 between Glasgow and Islay in place of a wooden paddle steamer named *Modern Athens*. The *Islay* sailed from Glasgow to Port Ellen on Mondays, then gave two return trips to West Loch Tarbert on the Kintyre Peninsula before returning to Glasgow on Fridays. In 1851 she extended her sailings to Skye and Lewis with a call at Oban. Described in advertisements as "powerful and fast-sailing", she was clipper-bowed, with two masts and one funnel abaft the paddle-boxes. She was bought in February 1868 by David Hutcheson, who renamed her *Dolphin* and placed her briefly on the Glasgow-Loch Fyne run, before selling her in July of the same year to Irish owners.

Right: The *Pioneer*, pictured in her original condition at Ballachulish Quarries *circa* 1859, had a long and distinguished career in the West Highlands, but like many of the early Hutcheson/MacBrayne steamers, she was not actually built for West Highland service. Launched on 4th June 1844 from the Paisley yard of Barr & McNab, she was an iron paddle steamer 159.8 feet long and 17.8 feet wide, with a draught of 8.8 feet and a gross tonnage of 144. She had a slanting stem (no bowsprit) and a single funnel abaft the paddle-boxes. The *Pioneer* was one of three vessels ordered for sailings to the Clyde Coast in connection with the newly formed Glasgow, Paisley and Greenock Railway, an early (though short-lived) example of a company running combined rail-and-steamer services. When the *Pioneer* first appeared on the Glasgow-Greenock-Rothesay route, she was the fastest boat on the river. The railway company soon lost interest in steamboat operation, and in 1847 its fleet was taken over by G. & J. Burns, whose shipping interests in the Western Isles passed in 1851 to David Hutcheson. Initially used by him on the Glasgow-Ardrishaig run, the *Pioneer* moved to Oban the following year for summer services to Crinan, Ballachulish, Fort William and Corpach.

This picture of the *Pioneer* at Oban *circa* 1869 shows the changes made to her appearance in the aftermath of an accident at Greenock in March 1862, when she ran aground and broke her back. Towed to Barclay Curle's yard for repair, she emerged with a beautiful clipper bow and gilt scroll work fore and aft. In 1868 feathering floats were installed, though she retained her large paddle-boxes, indicative of her original fixed-float condition. A mainmast was also added, only to be removed in 1872. Although not built for the Hutcheson/MacBrayne fleet, the *Pioneer* set a trend for the naming of their subsequent vessels, many of which shared the *–eer/ier* suffix.

The main interest here is not the private yacht anchored in the foreground but the steamer berthed beyond it at Oban's North Pier. This is the same *Pioneer* of 1844 as transformed by a major overhaul in 1874-5, during which she was given a straight stem and deck-saloons fore and aft of the paddle-boxes. The loss of her bowsprit was offset by the addition of a second funnel which, together with her lengthening by 27 feet, gave her a more impressive appearance. Her gross tonnage rose to 209. In this guise the *Pioneer* became best known on the Staffa and Iona excursion three days a week out of Oban, running to Fort William and Corpach on the other three. She also served on the Oban-Gairloch summer service and the Oban-Sound of Mull-Loch Sunart run. She was withdrawn in 1893 and sold for scrap in 1895.

The first *Mountaineer*, pictured late in her career in a crowded Oban Bay, was the first ship to be purpose-built for David Hutcheson. A product of the Clydebank yard of J. & G. Thomson (later known as John Brown & Co, builder of the Cunard *Queens*), she was designed as a replacement for the *Pioneer* on Hutcheson's Glasgow-Ardrishaig service, taking up the run in 1852. Three years later she was transferred to Oban, being employed on the Staffa/Iona summer excursion and the double-daily service to Fort William/Corpach. Originally flush-decked with a slanting, ornately decorated stem and a square stern, she was a fine specimen – a judgement that scarcely changed after she was lengthened and given deck saloons in 1876, as seen here. The *Mountaineer* had an ignominious end, stranding on the Lady Rock near the Lismore lighthouse in September 1889. She was little damaged, but bad weather set in before she could be salvaged and she broke in two. The crew were said to have saved her paddles, funnels and part of her machinery.

Opposite: Photographs of ships at St Kilda are rare. This one shows the *Clydesdale*, built at Clydebank in 1862 for David Hutcheson's Glasgow-Stornoway cargo and passenger service. After the arrival of the superior *Claymore* in 1881 the *Clydesdale* undertook the bi-weekly service from Glasgow to Islay and in 1883 was transferred to Skye, where she worked the daily mail service between Portree and Strome Ferry. In 1889 she began working from Oban to the Outer Hebrides, and it was during this period that she occasionally visited St Kilda. When she was reboilered in 1893 she received a second funnel. The *Clydesdale* met the same fate as the *Mountaineer*, stranding in January 1905 on the Lady Rock, an outcrop south of Lismore that is covered by water at high tide.

This is the earliest known photograph of a paddle steamer in the Outer Hebrides. Taken sometime between 1873 and 1875 it shows the *St Clair of the Isles* (left of centre, with tall slim funnel) at Stornoway on the Isle of Lewis. Built in 1860 by J. Reid & Co of Port Glasgow for Portuguese owners, who named her *Lisboa*, she was purchased in 1873 by the newly formed Western Isles Steam Packet Company, one of several early shipping ventures formed by Glasgow and Hebridean merchants to cater for the rapidly increasing trade to and from the islands. Reboilered, renamed and resplendent with a figurehead of a Highlander in full costume, the *St Clair of the Isles* plied a weekly service from Glasgow to the Western Isles. On her return to the Clyde from one such voyage in November 1873 she unloaded 70 head of cattle, 83 pigs, 10 tons of cheese, dried fish, lobsters, wool and 87 passengers. She had her fair share of breakdowns and groundings – not unusual for ships of her day plying in such treacherous waters – but was popular with the islanders. Sold in March 1875 to English owners, she was later reported to have voyaged as far afield as Singapore.

Where the *St Clair of the Isles* had blazed a trail, the *Dunara Castle* followed. After entering service in 1875 for Martin Orme & Co (later McCallum, Orme), she plied almost continuously for more than 70 years between Glasgow and the West Highlands, giving many communities not just a welcome point of contact with the outside world but a vital means of importing and exporting goods. Leaving Glasgow at midday on a Thursday and returning the following Wednesday, she stopped at Greenock Customhouse Quay to load more cargo before heading round the Mull of Kintyre to Colonsay, Iona, Bunessan on the west of Mull, Tiree and Coll, and then across the Minch to the Outer Hebrides. Among the outlying places she visited were Carbost in Skye, Loch Skipport in South Uist (where she is pictured, right) and Rodel in Harris. Once a month in summer the *Dunara Castle* would venture further west to St Kilda, carrying a complement of tourists eager to sample the varied delights of the Hebrides. Originally a two-funneller, she was remodelled with a single funnel in 1894, sailing on until 1948.

Before the advent of radar and other modern navigational aids, ships serving the Hebrides relied on their Masters' compass-work and local knowledge to guide them through the storms, mists and rocky passages for which these waters are renowned. Only in summer did boats like the *Dunara Castle* venture out as far as St Kilda, the evacuation of which she assisted in 1930. The *Dunara Castle* had a reputation as a fine sea boat but was not immune to the hazards of her trade: in adverse weather the sheltered waters of the Clyde could prove just as treacherous as the more exposed Minch. She is pictured aground at Battery Point, Greenock, on 29th August 1922.

The *Lochiel* was one of several all-year-round passenger and cargo boats ordered by David Hutcheson in the 1870s to bolster his services to the Western Isles. Built by A. & J. Inglis of Pointhouse, Glasgow, the *Lochiel* entered service in 1877, working initially on the Oban-Tobermory-Loch Sunart run and then the Islay service from West Loch Tarbert, where she is pictured. With her straight stem, single funnel and two masts, she was a functional-looking steamer that drew little attention to herself.

In the 1880s the *Lochiel* undertook services from the railhead at Strome Ferry to Portree and Stornoway. By the 1890s she was running from Skye to Lochmaddy in North Uist and Tarbert, Harris, where she is pictured unloading her cargo. Her end came in 1905 when she ran aground at Portree.

The Royal Route

The Royal Route was a connected transport system by sea and canal from Glasgow to Inverness, summer only, targeted at tourists, landowners, their guests and staff. It was so named because of a visit to the West Highlands in 1847 by Queen Victoria and Prince Albert. Growth of summer traffic on the route in the 1850s was so fast, and the section from Glasgow to Ardrishaig so crucial to its success, that each ship placed on the run lasted only a few years before being relegated to less important routes and replaced by a superior vessel. That had been the fate of the *Pioneer* and *Mountaineer*, but with the arrival of the first *Iona* in 1855, a new era in maritime splendour dawned on the Clyde.

A flush-decked paddler with curved bow, ornately decorated square stern, two funnels and single mast, the *Iona* was the finest ship of her day, setting a standard of sleekness, splendour and speed that was to become synonymous with the Clyde section of the Royal Route for the following one hundred years. After eight seasons the first *Iona* was sold to the Confederate States for blockade running during the American Civil War, but before she could leave the Clyde she collided with another ship off Gourock and sank. Her successor of 1863 was fitted with deck saloons but suffered a similar fate: sold for blockade running after only one season, she sank near Lundy Island as she set off across the Atlantic. A third *Iona*, closely modelled on her predecessor, entered service in 1864 and lasted 72 years in the MacBrayne fleet.

But the most enduring symbol of the Royal Route was the *Columba*, a paddler on a larger, more majestic scale than the *Iona*, with deckhouses extending the width of the ship. The *Columba* entered service on the Glasgow-Ardrishaig run in 1878 and continued every summer (with interruptions during the 1914-18 war) until 1935. As travel became faster, more sophisticated and more comfortable, the Royal Route established itself as the principal Society artery to the Highlands. It was the perfect marketing tool for the Hutcheson/MacBrayne fleet and its burgeoning network of land-and-sea tours, not just because of its royal associations, but because it embraced many of the best-known beauty spots of Scotland's West Coast.

Starting in the early morning at the Broomielaw in Glasgow, the steamer would sail down the River Clyde to Rothesay, calling at Greenock's Customhouse Quay, Princes Pier and others along the way. It then proceeded through the Kyles of Bute to Tarbert (for Islay) and Ardrishaig. At Ardrishaig passengers transferred to a canal boat for the second part of their journey – a nine-mile traversal of the Crinan Canal, taking them from the sheltered waters of the Clyde to the open sea at Crinan. In the early days of the Royal Route the canal boat was nothing more than a track-boat pulled by horses on the tow path. In 1866 a purpose-built vessel called the *Linnet* was introduced, making for a faster and more dignified trip. Joining the twin-funnelled *Chevalier* at Crinan in mid afternoon, passengers then journeyed north, stopping for the night at Oban or continuing to the head of Loch Linnhe. The following day they took another steamer from Banavie, at the southern end of the Caledonian Canal, through the locks and lochs of the Great Glen as far as Inverness.

At every step of the Royal Route, the steamer stopped at piers where the great and good, accompanied by their entourages, would alight and make the last part of their journey by horse-drawn carriage to the various Highland estates and hunting lodges. The quantity of luggage, bicycles and sporting equipment carried on the Royal Route had to be seen to be believed.

With the growing popularity of the motor car in the early decades of the 20th century, traffic on the Royal Route began to decline. After the loss of the *Chevalier* in 1927 and the withdrawal of the *Linnet* in 1929, MacBrayne's axed the Ardrishaig-Crinan-Oban boat connection. Steamer services on the Caledonian Canal continued until the outbreak of the Second World War. The Ardrishaig mail run survived until 1970, starting at Wemyss Bay during the Second World War and thereafter Gourock, and terminating at Tarbert in winter.

In its late 19th and early 20th century heyday, the Royal Route helped to turn the Highlands into an up-market holiday destination. David MacBrayne's 'swift steamers', with their fine lines, carved stems, red and black funnels and high standards of service, were the Royal Route's mark of quality – and its best advertisement.

The first part of the Royal Route ended halfway up Loch Fyne at Ardrishaig, where the *Iona* of 1864 is pictured. The third Hutcheson steamer to bear that name in quick succession, she sailed on the Ardrishaig run until the arrival of the *Columba* in 1878, and was thereafter placed on a variety of Clyde and West Highland routes, often supplementing the *Columba*. The *Iona* notched up a total of 72 years' service before she and the *Columba* were sold for breaking up at Dalmuir in 1935.

The *Columba* is widely regarded – even today, by people who never saw her – as the finest steamer ever to have plied the waters of the Clyde. Built, like the *Iona* and several other Hutcheson/MacBrayne paddlers, by J. & G. Thomson of Clydebank, she had a steel hull, at that time an experimental feature, with ornamented curved bow and a cylindrical design of paddle-box, with radial vents in black and gold and a thistle emanating from the letter 'U' of the ship's name. At 301 feet, the *Columba* was the longest ship ever built to serve the Clyde and Western Isles – though she never ventured beyond the Clyde. At the start and end of the season the *Columba* undertook occasional charter sailings, including one in 1885 from Greenock to Inveraray. During the 1914-18 war the starting point for the Ardrishaig service was Wemyss Bay. The *Columba* was in steam for barely four months every summer, spending the rest of the year in Bowling Harbour.

Apart from her length and fine looks, the *Columba* boasted several features that distinguished her from other Clyde steamers. Next to the engine room she had a post office: by the mid 1880s it was handling more than 80,000 letters and 400 telegrams per season (it was discontinued after the 1914-18 war). The dining saloon boasted a series of paintings by W. J. Keir illustrating old Scots sayings: installed when the steamer was launched in 1878, they remained in their original glass casings till her demise in 1935. Keir's stained glass work on the staircase leading to the saloon (a large window depicting St Columba landing on Iona) was saved from the breakers and last surfaced at auction in Glasgow in 1964. There was also a book stall, a fruit stall and a barber shop, latterly manned by 'Felix', who would show members of the crew letters he had received from American tourists years after he had attended to them, asking for his special hair tonic to be sent on.

The *Columba's* arrival at Tarbert around midday turned an otherwise sleepy pier on the shores of Loch Fyne into a bustle of activity, as all manner of luggage and mails were offloaded. For passengers on the Royal Route, Tarbert offered the first scent of the Hebrides. Those heading for Gigha, Islay and Jura would disembark and make the short journey to West Loch Tarbert on foot or by horse-drawn carriage, there to continue on one of the less exalted members of the Hutcheson/MacBrayne fleet. The *Columba* continued to Ardrishaig, where she disgorged the remainder of her complement, and passengers from the north boarded for the journey back to Glasgow. It was a quick turn-round: the *Columba* would return to Tarbert at 1.40pm, picking up passengers who had come from Islay in the morning, before heading through the Kyles of Bute and back up-river to Glasgow, reached shortly before 7pm. Exactly 12 hours later, the journey would begin again – a ritual performed daily except Sundays every summer for more than 50 years.

The *Linnet* sits at Ardrishaig, her easternmost berth on the Crinan Canal. From 1866 to 1929 she was integral to the package marketed by MacBrayne as the Royal Route. However quaint she may seem in retrospect, with her chimney-like funnel and a canoe-shaped bow to nose her way through lock gates, the *Linnet* represented a significant upgrade to West Highland travel in the 1860s. Over the following 60 years she carried hundreds of thousands of visitors, berthing each night at Crinan and setting off for Ardrishaig after the arrival at 10am of the twin-funnelled *Chevalier* from Oban and the north. Reaching Ardrishaig in time for the *Columba's* arrival shortly before 1pm, she then retraced her journey to Crinan, where the *Chevalier* would be waiting to take passengers on the next stage of the Royal Route to Oban, Fort William and Corpach. In winter the *Linnet* was laid up under cover near Cairnbaan. This picture was taken before 1894, when a navigating bridge and deckhouse were added.

In this view of Crinan the *Linnet* sits at her canal berth to the right of centre while the *Chevalier* prepares to head north on the next stage of the Royal Route. The *Chevalier* was one of three memorable MacBrayne steamers dating from 1866: the others were the *Linnet* on the Crinan Canal and the *Gondolier* on the Caledonian Canal. All of them served their owner for more than 60 years. The *Chevalier* was the first to go, the victim of paddle-wheel trouble near Tarbert during a gale in March 1927, while on one of her winter spells on the Ardrishaig mail run. She drifted onto rocks, took in water and was deemed not worth repairing. She was broken up at Troon.

The journey from Crinan took the steamer through the Dorus Mor to Blackmill Bay on the island of Luing and then to Easdale, where the *Chevalier* is pictured negotiating the narrow approach to the pier, the remains of which are visible today. You can only marvel at how the *Chevalier's* skipper manoeuvred his boat through this treacherously rocky passage in fair weather and foul. The *Chevalier* was originally intended for the Staffa and Iona excursion from Oban, but in 1886 moved to the Crinan run, with which she became closely identified for the rest of her career. She would berth overnight at Corpach at the head of Loch Linnhe, leaving shortly after 5am on a journey that included stops at Fort William, Corran, Onich, Ballachulish, Appin and Oban, reaching Crinan at 10am. Leaving again at 3pm, she was due at Corpach at 7.30 in the evening.

The *Chevalier's* long lie at Crinan in the middle of the day gave her crew ample time to keep her clean. Many of them returned to her season after season, and took great pride in their ship. She was a delight to the eye, with graceful hull, flaming red funnels and polished copper steam pipes, gleaming in the sun. This picture shows the *Chevalier's* main saloon aft, after the installation of electric light in 1919-20. The staircase on the bottom right corner led to a dining saloon at water level.

The northward sail up Loch Linnhe from Oban, offering some of the most scenic views in the West Highlands, includes a passage through the tidal race at Corran Narrows, where the *Iona* is pictured heading back south late in her career. After the *Columba* took over the Ardrishaig mail service in 1878, the *Iona* took up the Corpach-Crinan run until 1886, when she returned to the Clyde, playing second fiddle to the *Columba* and deputising for her at the start and end of the season. In the early 1920s she found new employment on a sailing from Glasgow to Lochgoilhead and Arrochar, before returning to West Highland waters in 1928, serving mainly on the Oban-Fort William run.

After calling at Fort William, the steamer proceeded to Corpach at the entrance to Loch Eil, where the southern end of the Caledonian Canal joins the sea. Until 1895 passengers on the Royal Route transferred at Corpach, under the shadow of Ben Nevis, to horse-drawn carriages that took them up Neptune's Staircase – a steep flight of canal locks – to Banavie, where another paddle steamer was waiting to take them to Inverness. The steamer in this view of Corpach is the *Grenadier* of 1885, a rare visitor to the head of Loch Linnhe. Latterly the connection from Fort William to Banavie was made by train.

The final part of the Royal Route took visitors the entire length of the Great Glen, from Banavie to Inverness. It began with an eight and a half mile uninterrupted passageway, parallel to the River Lochy, as far as the entrance to Loch Lochy (10 miles long), followed by Loch Oich (three and a half miles). The steamer then proceeded through a flight of locks at Fort Augustus, before entering Loch Ness (23 miles). Steaming north-east towards Inverness, there would be calls at Invermoriston, Foyers, Inverfarigaig and Temple. The steamer most associated with this journey was the *Gondolier*, pictured entering Loch Ness at Fort Augustus (with one of her consorts, the *Glengarry*, in the background). Built in 1866, the *Gondolier* spent more than 70 years plying back and forth along the Caledonian Canal in summer. Winter refits were usually carried out at Inverness, though she returned to the Clyde for more extensive reconditioning.

The *Gondolier*, pictured (left) at Muirtown near Inverness, in August 1899, was the flagship of the Hutcheson/MacBrayne fleet on the Caledonian Canal. Sailing in summer months between the northern and southern ends of the Canal, she left Muirtown Wharf, Inverness, at 7am on Mondays, Wednesdays and Fridays, and spent the best part of a day negotiating the lochs and locks on the single journey to Banavie, which she reached around 3.30pm. Passengers could then walk or take a coach past Neptune's Staircase to the pier at Corpach, where the 3.50 steamer to Oban awaited them. Returning to Inverness on Tuesdays, Thursdays and Saturdays, the *Gondolier* would leave Banavie at 9.30am, reaching Inverness at 6.15pm. The steamer behind the *Gondolier* is the *Ethel*. Built in 1880 in Ireland and originally employed there, she became a MacBrayne boat in 1885, serving mainly on the Glasgow-Inverness cargo route until 1915, and later on the Stornoway run until she foundered at sea in 1924.

It took the *Gondolier* about 45 minutes to negotiate the canal locks at Fort Augustus. This gave travellers on the Royal Route one of their most pleasurable experiences: they could disembark, visit the College and Cloisters of the Benedictine Abbey, or watch the various manoeuvres that took the steamer through to the next level. This photograph shows the *Gondolier* in the 1930s, after the fitting of a new, thicker funnel and the enlargement of her saloon windows. By this time she was the sole surviving steamer on the canal, traffic having fallen considerably since the 1914-18 war. The *Gondolier* was finally withdrawn in 1939 and taken over by the Admiralty, her hull being subsequently used to block one of the passages at Scapa Flow. She was never replaced.

Dochgarroch Lock was the only lock that canal steamers had to negotiate between Muirtown Wharf at Inverness and the entrance to Loch Ness. The lockmen – helped by the crew and, to judge by this turn-of-century postcard, any passing dogs that cared to lend a paw – opened the locks by pushing long poles fixed into an enormous screw linking the lock-gates on both sides. The steamer here is the *Lochness*, built in 1853 as the *Lochgoil* for the Loch Goil Company. She had a chequered career on the Clyde and at Londonderry before being bought in 1885 by David MacBrayne, who shortened her, gave her deck saloons and employed her for the next 27 years on the mail run from Inverness to Fort Augustus.

This steamer was already 34 years old when she joined MacBrayne's canal fleet in 1894 with a new name, the *Gairlochy*. Built in 1861 as the *Sultan*, she was originally a flush-decked ship, serving various owners on the Clyde, latterly under the name of *Ardmore*. MacBrayne shortened her hull, added a saloon and fitted a canoe-like bow similar to the *Gondolier* for easy negotiation of the canal locks – turning her into the most attractive of the paddlers on the Caledonian Canal. Named after a village at the southern end of Loch Lochy, the *Gairlochy* enjoyed another quarter-century in service, operating as the *Gondolier's* opposite number between Banavie and Inverness, until she was destroyed by fire at Fort Augustus in December 1919.

The *Glengarry*, pictured at Muirtown Wharf in the early 1880s, was the oldest and longest-serving of MacBrayne's steamers on the Caledonian Canal. Built on the Clyde in 1844 as the *Edinburgh Castle*, she was transferred to the canal in 1846, passing into David Hutcheson's ownership in 1851. In 1875 she was lengthened, modernised and given the name that was to last her until her withdrawal in 1927, by which time she was reckoned to be the oldest steamer in the world. Until the arrival of the *Gairlochy* in 1894, the *Glengarry* partnered the *Gondolier* on the Inverness-Banavie run: travelling in opposite directions, the two steamers would usually meet at Cullochy Lock at the north end of Loch Oich, the highest point of the journey. For the last part of her career the *Glengarry* was confined to the mail run between Inverness and Fort Augustus.

Though not part of the Royal Route, steamboat sailings to Staffa and Iona were an important adjunct to it. When steamers started visiting them in the 1820s, the romantic allure of these remote islands was already well-known, thanks to the literary efforts of authors as diverse as Samuel Johnson, Walter Scott and John Keats. The composer Felix Mendelssohn, the poet William Wordsworth and the painter J. M. W. Turner soon followed, and by the 1860s the 'Sacred Isles Tour' was an essential part of the tourist trail. This picture shows the MacBrayne paddle steamer *Gael* anchored off Fingal's Cave at Staffa – probably in 1903, the only year this steamer is known to have been used on the Round Mull excursion. MacBrayne's continued to advertise a visit to Staffa until 1967, when there was a rock fall at Fingal's Cave – after which insurance cover became prohibitive. The Staffa call was devised in the days when the steamer would have up to 200 on board: landing by small boats could be undertaken in reasonable time before the steamer proceeded to Iona, where the same genteel process was used to ferry passengers ashore. By the 1950s up to 800 would undertake the trip on a good day, making two such landings increasingly impractical, and the rock fall at Staffa came as a blessing to MacBrayne's. Thereafter the steamer passed Staffa slowly, stopping off Fingal's Cave to let everyone have a view before proceeding to Iona.

Until the arrival of the turbine *King George V* in 1936, the ship most closely associated with summer sailings to Staffa and Iona was the *Grenadier*. She was one of MacBrayne's most graceful steamers, with clipper bow, bowsprit, two red-and-black funnels and saloons the width of the hull. She is pictured at Iona before 1901, when a new set of boilers was installed and her original slim funnels were replaced by stouter versions. She often served as the winter relief on the Ardrishaig mail run and had a reputation as a good sea boat. Her end came suddenly in September 1927, when she was gutted by fire at Oban's North Pier with the loss of several of her crew.

The Coming of Rail

Until the 1880s the most practical way to move round the West Highlands was by sea. Roads hardly existed; transport by horse and carriage was unreliable and uncomfortable. Sea journeys could be slow but they were regular. Speed of access was never the priority: maintaining commercial links was, as much for island folk wanting to get their goods to mainland markets as for traders selling modern merchandise to the islands.

The arrival of rail changed all that. Railways made the West Highlands more accessible, in much the same way that car ferries were to revolutionise links to the islands in the late 20th century. The traditional way of visiting and provisioning the Hebrides – by sea from Glasgow round the Mull of Kintyre – held good for a while, but with the coming of rail Highland life started to speed up. Railheads became steamer-hubs, opening up the islands' economy and boosting tourism. Journey times from Skye and Mull to Glasgow were halved.

The first railway-and-steamer operation in the West Highlands, at Strome Ferry in Loch Carron in 1870, did not take off as expected: the Dingwall & Skye Railway tried to run its own steamer fleet but lacked the expertise. The real breakthrough came with the completion of the Callander & Oban Railway's line to Oban in 1880, creating opportunities that David MacBrayne was quick to exploit. The North British Railway Company's line from Glasgow to Fort William followed in 1894. In 1897 the Highland Railway reached Kyle of Lochalsh (below), supplanting the previous terminus at Strome Ferry and leading to the same expansion of steamer services that had earlier been seen at Oban. Finally, in 1901, the Fort William line was extended 45 miles north-westwards to the fishing village of Mallaig, creating what has been recognised ever since as one of the most scenic railway journeys in the United Kingdom.

All this impacted not just on tourists, travellers and traders but ship owners – especially David MacBrayne, by 1880 the dominant force in West Highland shipping. Broadly speaking, MacBrayne's fleet divided into two types of ship – the 'swift steamers' carrying passengers, mail and goods from Oban and other coastal ports, and the 'all-the-way steamers' from Glasgow, which concentrated on cargo and livestock, though not to the exclusion of passengers. It was the 'swift steamers' – sturdy paddlers like the *Grenadier* and *Fusilier*, with handsome lines and daytime sailings – that were to profit most from the coming of rail, leaving their 'all-the-way' consorts with the less rewarding but more essential services.

Oban before the coming of rail

When the railway came to Oban the whole shape of the harbour changed: an elaborate railhead was established on the south side of the bay, flanked by a new wharf appropriately named the Railway Pier. Oban was already the base for services up Loch Linnhe to Fort William, a mail run through the Sound of Mull to Tobermory and Loch Sunart and, in summer, tourist sailings to Crinan, Iona and Staffa. With the journey time from Glasgow to Oban reduced from 16 hours by sea to four by rail, MacBrayne began to run services in connection with the railway, and the volume of traffic out of Oban increased, with steamers arriving and leaving at all times of the day.

One of the new services was a three-times-a-week summer sailing that linked Oban with Skye and Gairloch on the Wester Ross mainland. Leaving Oban on Tuesdays, Thursdays and Saturdays at 7am, the steamer headed up the Sound of Mull, calling at Craignure, Lochaline, Salen and Tobermory, and proceeded round Ardnamurchan Point to Eigg and Arisaig (Mallaig from 1901) and up the Sound of Sleat to Kyle of Lochalsh (from 1897), Broadford and Portree, before crossing back to the mainland and spending the night at Gairloch. The return trip was on Mondays, Wednesdays and Fridays. It was a fabulously scenic voyage. Travellers could do a circular trip, returning to Oban by coach from Gairloch to Achnasheen, train to Inverness, then steamer through the Caledonian Canal and down Loch Linnhe. Later, as traffic through Mallaig and Kyle increased, the Oban-Gairloch run lost its rationale. It dropped from the schedule after the 1914-18 war.

The coming of rail had other, more workaday repercussions for Hebridean steamer services. The UK government, taking a closer interest in the welfare of the islanders, offered new mail contracts, which David MacBrayne snapped up, taking his ships into territory that had traditionally been the preserve of McCallum and Orme. By 1891 MacBrayne had added four steamers to the fleet operating from Oban's Railway Pier – the *Fingal, Flowerdale, Gael* and *Staffa*. The Inner and Outer Islands service was recast and now required three steamers – one for Coll and Tiree and two for a circuit linking Barra, Benbecula, the Uists, Skye, Canna and Rum. It was boom time for Oban – and for MacBrayne's.

Oban's Railway Pier (right of centre), with its station and extensive sidings, was built on reclaimed land round the bay from the North Pier (upper left). Passenger and cargo steamers for the islands used the Railway Pier; mail and excursion steamers used the North Pier. The vessel in the foreground at the Railway Pier is the *Hebrides*, a McCallum Orme all-the-way ship that stopped at Oban on her way from Glasgow to the islands. The *Fusilier*, one of MacBrayne's swift steamers, lies at the North Pier. Although David MacBrayne had sent the *Iona* round from the Clyde to Oban to join in the Railway Pier's opening celebrations in 1880, his initial concern was that the railway might encroach on his trade. As traffic to the islands boomed, however, he quickly saw it as a business opportunity.

Protected from the open sea by the island of Kerrera, Oban had always offered seafarers a natural haven, where private yachts would congregate in summer. The coming of rail in the late 19th century turned it into the 'Charing Cross of the Highlands', with steamers arriving and leaving at all times of the day. This picture of the North Pier, dating from shortly before the 1914-18 war, gives an indication of the variety of vessels working out of Oban. To the left lies the *Lochinvar*, the Tobermory mail steamer; next comes the *Grenadier*, the Iona and Staffa boat; then the *Chevalier*, whose run linked Corpach and Crinan; and to the right is the *Chieftain*, MacBrayne's Glasgow-based cruise steamer.

The first Highland railhead to be established with a steamer service was at Strome Ferry in Loch Carron, which the Dingwall & Skye Railway, a subsidiary of the Highland Railway, reached in 1870. Connections were made by steamer to Portree and Stornoway, but the service, operated by the railway owners, was so unsatisfactory that David MacBrayne was persuaded to take it over in 1880, initially using the *Lochiel* and *Glencoe*. This picture predates the MacBrayne takeover, and shows the *Carham* at Strome Ferry sometime during the decade (1870-80) when she was based there. Built in 1864 for service on the Solway Firth, and later owned by G. & J. Burns, the *Carham* was a paddle steamer with funnel abaft the paddle-boxes. She ended her days in English waters and was scrapped in 1888.

This picture of Kyle of Lochalsh Pier in November 1897 shows the two MacBrayne boats that inaugurated steamer services from the new railhead – the *Lovedale* and *Gael*. Both were ships that David MacBrayne had imported from south-west England. The *Lovedale* (foreground) was acquired in 1891 from the Great Western Railway, which had employed her (as *Great Western*) on cross-channel services to France and Ireland. Placed on MacBrayne's Strome Ferry-Stornoway service, she was considerably altered (and renamed) during a refit in 1893, when her two funnels were replaced by one, placed too far aft to give a nicely balanced profile. She was broken up in 1904. The *Gael*, the two-funnelled steamer at the end of the pier, was at that time employed on the Oban-Portree-Gairloch route.

The final rail terminus to be established on the west coast, in 1901, was Mallaig, which became the base for MacBrayne's services to the Outer Hebrides. This photo dates from very soon after the opening of the pier, at that time little more than a protective harbour wall surrounded by thatched fishermen's cottages. The steamer at the quay is the *Clydesdale* of 1861 in her two-funnel guise. The railway rapidly expanded the local economy and gave a huge boost to the fishing industry in the area. The new harbour was closer to the rich fishing grounds west of Barra than either of the other railheads at Oban and Kyle of Lochalsh, and fishermen were quick to exploit the possibility of getting their catch to metropolitan markets faster. Before long Mallaig Harbour was being used by many more vessels than had been expected. Extensions to the wharf began almost immediately. A hotel was built and the community expanded round the bay.

The *Gael* at Portree. Between 1892 and 1902 the *Gael* spent her summers on the Oban-Portree-Gairloch run, latterly including a call at Mallaig; in winter she proved useful on relief duty elsewhere. She was not the most beautiful of Hebridean boats but she had one of the most varied careers. Built in 1867 for the Campbeltown and Glasgow Company, she was sold to the Great Western Railway Company in 1883 for its Bristol Channel, Scilly Isles and Channel Islands services. After her acquisition by MacBrayne in 1891 she was reboilered and remodelled, with her cargo hold and mainmast removed and a full-breadth aft saloon added. She undertook the Staffa and Iona excursion in 1903, and was occasionally used on the winter Ardrishaig mail service and the Stornoway run, and even on the Ardrossan-Arran service in 1919. A raised fo'c'sle was added in the early 1900s. She was broken up in 1924.

Kentallen, on the eastern shore of Loch Linnhe, was unusual in having both a railway and steamer connection to Oban in the first three decades of the 20th century. The railway, built in the late 1890s to carry slate from the Ballachulish Quarries, ran from Connel Ferry across Lochs Etive and Creran to Appin, Kentallen, Ballachulish Ferry and Ballachulish. The pier was served by MacBrayne's steamer – here the *Fusilier* – on the run between Oban and Fort William. Built in 1888 by McArthur of Paisley, the 'Fusey' was one of the most versatile vessels in the fleet, operating in various capacities on the Clyde, at Oban and on the Mallaig-Kyle-Portree mail service.

The beauty and detail of a MacBrayne paddler's scrollwork is well profiled in this view of the *Fusilier* (right) in Greenock's East India Harbour. The picture dates from around 1930, after the *Fusilier* had undergone modifications that gave her an enlarged funnel, with the bridge placed in front. She was a maid of all work – a smaller, single-funnelled version of the *Grenadier*, almost as pretty to look at but unspectacular in speed. In 1934 she was sold for excursion sailings on the Forth. She remained there for only one season, ending her days sailing out of Ramsgate on the south coast of England and Llandudno in Wales, where she had the name *Lady Orme*. She was broken up in 1939. The ship on the left is the *Lochshiel*, a useful little boat built in 1929 for MacBrayne's cargo run from Glasgow to the Firth of Lorne, Mull, Loch Sunart and Loch Leven. She was sold in 1952 and broken up in Belgium in 1955.

Towards the end of the 19th century MacBrayne faced a pressing need for new tonnage – partly to replace an ageing fleet but also in response to increased demand. After the commissioning of the *Fusilier* in 1888, several ships were bought second-hand – though even some of these were hardly in the first flush of youth. Among them was the second *Mountaineer*, seen here in Oban Bay. Built in 1858 as the *Hero* for service on the Clyde, she had been bought by MacBrayne in 1890 as a temporary replacement for the *Iona* on the up-firth run from Ardrishaig. Two years later she underwent a transformation that turned her from an unexceptional steamer into a beauty, with clipper bow and bowsprit. Based at Oban in summer, she ran on various excursion routes. In 1893, for example, she was advertised as departing Oban at 9am on Mondays, Wednesdays and Fridays for Craignure, Lochaline, Salen, Tobermory, Salen (Loch Sunart) and Strontian, returning to Oban at 6pm. She was sold for scrap in 1909.

Another of the 'new' acquisitions was the *Carabinier*, pictured at Salen in Loch Sunart. Built at Southampton in 1878 as the *Albert Edward*, she was unusual for a MacBrayne boat in that she had never been in Scottish waters until she was bought in 1893. A neat but unspectacular little steamer with a cargo derrick on her single mast, she carried passengers, mails and cargo all-year-round on the Oban-Tobermory-Loch Sunart service. She was broken up at Troon in 1908.

Serving the Islands

The 1880s and 1890s saw a rapid expansion of David MacBrayne's Hebridean empire, thanks partly to business generated by the new railheads and partly to MacBrayne's assumption of the mail contract for thrice weekly services to Coll, Tiree, Barra and South Uist – islands that had previously been served only on a weekly basis by the ships of John McCallum and Martin Orme. But while the fleet grew apace at the various railheads, 'all-the-way' sailings from Glasgow continued to form the backbone of the islands' steamer service.

The McCallum and Orme boats – *Dunara Castle* (below at Bunessan, Mull), *Hebridean* and *Hebrides* – were as much a part of island life as MacBrayne's *Claymore* and *Clansman*, and remained so until the 1940s. But it was these two 'all-the-way' steamers that carried the most traffic, one leaving on Monday, the other on Thursday. Heading off down the Clyde at 1pm on their weekly voyage to Stornoway they called at 20 different ports *en route*, starting with Greenock's Customhouse Quay. They would round the Mull of Kintyre overnight, before spending an hour or two discharging cargo at Oban around 8am. The ships then called briefly at Craignure, Lochaline and Salen, and spent an hour or so at Tobermory. After passing Ardnamurchan Point they would make brief stops on either side of the Sound of Sleat, arriving at Portree by mid evening. Early next morning they would cross to Wester Ross – Aultbea, Gairloch, Loch Clash, Lochinver, Poolewe, Totaig, Ullapool, though not all on the same trip – before braving the Minch to Stornoway. The Thursday boat would spend Sunday in the Lewis port before retracing her steps, usually with one or two variations, reaching Glasgow again on Wednesday. The Monday steamer, not being subject to the Sabbath, would do a quicker turn-round at Stornoway and sometimes visit Tarbert, Harris, and Lochmaddy before heading back to Portree.

MacBrayne's timetables listed departure times for all ports of call but advised passengers that "The hours noted above are not to be relied upon – they only show the average sailing time. The Steamer may be earlier or later than what is stated". Martin Orme's timetables were even less specific. No timings were given for the journey north, and departures on the return were stated as "about" 4am or 6pm – an indication of how leisurely time-keeping was in the Hebrides a century ago, when life followed its own unhurried pace.

A vivid description of a late 19th century Hebridean steamer journey was given by the Scottish poet Alexander Smith in *A Summer in Skye*. He recounts his return voyage from Portree to Glasgow aboard the first steamer to bear the name *Clansman*, built in 1855 and wrecked in 1869. Though written in 1864 (and abridged here), the scenes he recalls were repeated time and again over the following half-century. The 'hurricane deck' to which Smith refers was a small platform-like top deck (seen here on the *Hebridean*), from which passengers could gain an elevated view of their surroundings.

The 'Clansman' reached Portree at 11pm, and I went on board at once and went to bed. When I awoke next morning, we were steaming down the Sound of Raasay; and when breakfast-time arrived, it needed but a glance to discover that autumn had come and that the sporting season was well-nigh over. A lot of sheep were penned up near the bows, amidships were piles of wool, groups of pointers and setters were scattered about, and at the breakfast-table were numerous sportsmen returning to the south, whose conversation ran on grouse-shooting, salmon fishing, and deer-stalking. While breakfast was proceeding you saw everywhere sun-browned faces, heard cheery voices, and witnessed the staying of prodigious appetites. Before these stalwart fellows steaks, chops, platefuls of ham and eggs disappeared as if by magic.

The breakfast party, too, consisted of all orders and degrees of men. There were drovers going to, or returning from markets; merchants from Stornoway going south; a couple of Hebridean clergymen; several military men of frank and hearty bearing; an extensive brewer; three members of Parliament; and a tall and handsome English Earl of some repute on the turf. Several ladies, too, dropped in before the meal was over. We were all hungry, and fed like Homer's heroes. When breakfast was over we all went up stairs; the smoking men resorted to the hurricane deck, the two clergymen read, the merchants from Stornoway wandered uneasily about as if seeking some one to whom they could attach themselves, and the drovers smoked short pipes amidships, and when their pipes were out went forward to examine the sheep.

The morning and forenoon wore away and there were frequent stoppages, and the villages on the shore, the coming and going of boats with cargo and passengers, the throwing out of empty barrels here, the getting in of wool there, were incidents quite worthy of the regard of idle men leading for the time being a mere life of the senses. We stopped for a couple of hours in Broadford Bay – we stopped at Kyleakin – we stopped at Balmacara; and the long-looked-for dinner was served after we had past Kyle-Rhea, and were gliding down into Glenelg.

For some little time previously savoury steams had assailed our nostrils. We saw the stewards descending into the cabin with covered dishes, and at the first sound of the bell the hurricane deck, crowded a moment before, was left entirely empty. The captain took his seat at the head of the table with a mighty roast before him, the clergyman said grace – somewhat lengthily, in the opinion of most – the covers were lifted away by deft waiters, and we dined that day at four as if we had not previously breakfasted at eight, and lunched at one.

In autumn frequently the steamer has to leave her direct course and thread long inland running lochs to take wool on board. These stoppages and wanderings would be annoying if you were hurrying south to be married, or if you were summoned to the deathbed of a friend from whom you had expectations; but as it is holiday with you, and as every divergence brings you into unexpected scenery, they are regarded rather as a pleasure than anything else. When we reached the top [of Loch Nevis] there was an immense to-do on the beach; some three or four boats laden with wool were already pulling out towards the steamer, which immediately lay to and let off noisy steam; men were tumbling bales of wool into the empty boats that lay at the stony pier, and to the pier laden carts were hurrying down from the farm-house that stood remote. The wool boats came on either side of the steamer; doors were opened in the bulwarks, to these doors steam cranes were wheeled, and with many a shock of crank and rattle of loosened chain, the bales were hoisted on deck and consigned to the gloomy recesses of the hold. As soon as a boat was emptied, a laden one pulled out to take its place; the steam cranes were kept continually jolting and rattling, and in the space of a couple of hours a considerable amount of business had been done.

On the present occasion the transference of wool from the boats to the hold of the steamer occupied a longer time than was usual; sunset had come in crimson and died away to pale gold and rose, and still the laden boats came slowly on, and still the steam cranes were at their noisy work. The whole affair, having by this time lost all sense of novelty, was in danger of becoming tiresome, but in the fading light the steward had lighted up the saloon into hospitable warmth and glow, and then the bell rang for tea. In a moment all interest in the wool boats had come to an end, the passengers hurried below, and before the tinklings of cup and saucer had ceased, the last bale of wool had been transferred from the boats alongside to the hold, and the 'Clansman' had turned round, and was softly gliding down Loch Nevis.

A lovely, transparent autumn night arched above us, a young moon and single star by her side, when we reached Arisaig. By this time the ladies had retired, and those of the gentlemen who remained on deck were wrapped in plaids, each shadowy figure brought out more keenly by the red tip of a cigar. The entrance into Arisaig is difficult, and the 'Clansman' was put on half steam. The gentlemen were requested to leave the hurricane deck, and there the captain stationed himself, while a couple of men were sent to the bows, and three or four stationed at the wheel. Slowly the large vessel moved onward, with low black reefs of rocks on either side, like smears of dark colour, but perfectly soft and tender in outline; and every here and there we could see the dark top of a rock peering out of the dim sea like a beaver's head. From these shadowy reefs, as the vessel moved on, the sea-birds were awaked from their slumbers, and strangely sweet, and liquid as flute-notes, were their cries and signals of alarm.

The passengers leaned against the bulwarks watching rock and sea, when suddenly there was a muffled shout from the outlook at the bows. The captain shouted 'Port! port! Hard!' and away went the wheel spinning, the stalwart fellows toiling at the spokes, and the ship slowly falling off. After a little while there was another noise at the bows, the captain shouted 'starboard!' and the wheel was rapidly reversed. We were now well up the difficult channel; and looking back we could see a perfect intricacy of reefs and dim single rocks behind, and a fading belt of pallor wandering amongst them, which told the track of the ship. After a while a low line of coast became visible, then a light broke upon it; and we beheld a dozen boats approaching, with lights at their bows. These were the Arisaig boats, laden with cargo. At sight of them the captain left the hurricane deck, the anchor went away with a thundering chain, the passengers went to bed, and between asleep and awake, I could hear half the night the trampling of feet, the sound of voices, and the jolt of the steam cranes, as the Arisaig goods were being hoisted on deck and stowed away.

I was up early next morning. Skye was perfectly visible, Eigg rose opposite, Muck lay ahead. The 'Clansman' soon reached the open sea, and we began to feel the impulse of the Atlantic. By the time the passengers began to appear on deck the ship was lurching heavily along towards the far-stretching headland of Ardnamurchan. It was difficult to keep one's feet steady – more difficult to keep steady one's brain. Great glittering watery mounds came heaving on, to wash with unavailing foam the rocky coast; and amongst these the steamer rolled and tossed and groaned, its long dark pennon of smoke streaming with the impulse of the sea.

The greater proportion of the passengers crawled amidships – beside the engines and the cook's quarters, which were redolent with the scent of herrings frying for a most unnecessary breakfast – for there the motion was least felt. To an unhappy landsman that morning the whole world seemed topsy-turvy. There was no straight line to be discovered anywhere; everything seemed to have changed places. But with all this turmoil and dancing and rolling, the 'Clansman' went swiftly on, and in due time we were off the Ardnamurchan lighthouse and were steaming towards Tobermory.

The longest delay during the passage is at Oban but then we had dinner there, which helped to kill the time in a pleasant way. The 'Clansman' had received a quantity of cargo at Tobermory, at Loch Aline a flock of sheep were driven on board, goods were taken in plentifully at other places in the Sound at which we touched, and when we had received all the stuffs waiting for us at Oban, the vessel was heavily laden. The entire steerage deck was a bellowing and bleating mass of black cattle and sheep, each 'parcel' divided from the other by temporary barriers. The space amidships was a chaos of barrels and trunks and bales of one kind or another, and amongst these the steerage passengers were forced to dispose themselves. Great piles of wooden boxes containing herring were laid along the cabin deck, so that if a man were disposed to walk about it behoved him to take care of his footsteps.

But who cared! We were away from Oban now, the wind was light, the sun setting behind us, and the bell ringing for tea. It was the last meal we were to have together, and through some consciousness of this the ice of reserve seemed to melt, and the passengers to draw closer to each other. Tea was prolonged after this pleasant fashion, and then, while the Stornoway merchants and the cattle-dealers solaced themselves with a tumbler of punch, the majority of the other passengers went up stairs to the hurricane deck to smoke. Slowly the night fell around the smokers, the stars came out in the soft sky, as the air grew chill, and one by one they went below. Then there was more toddy-drinking, some playing at chess, one or two attempts at letter-writing, and at eleven o'clock the waiters cleared the tables, and began to transform the saloon into a large sleeping apartment.

I climbed up to my berth and fell comfortably asleep. [When I awoke] the ship was labouring heavily. I slipped out of bed, and, steadying myself for a favourable moment, made a grab at my clothes. Then I staggered on deck. Holding on by the first support, I was almost blinded by the glare of broken seas. From a high coast against which the great waves rushed came the steady glare of a lighthouse, and by that token I knew we were 'on' the Mull of Cantyre. The ship was fuming through a mighty battle of tides. Shadowy figures of steerage passengers were to be seen clinging here and there. One – a young woman going to Glasgow as a housemaid, as she afterwards told me – was in great distress, under the impression that we were all going to the bottom. Once when the ship made a wild lurch, and a cloud of spray came flying over the deck, she exclaimed to a sailor who was shuffling past wearing a sou'wester and canvas overalls, 'O sailor, is't ever sae bad as this?'. Happily the turmoil was not of long duration. In an hour we had rounded the formidable Mull, had reached comparatively smooth water, and with the lights of Campbelton behind, I went below again, and slept till we reached Greenock.

The *Clansman* of 1870 at Lochinver

The *Clansman* of 1870 reverses out of the pier at Loch Clash near Kinlochbervie, just south of Cape Wrath on the Sutherland coast. Until the First World War the Glasgow-Stornoway steamer made regular calls at remote communities on the north-west corner of the Scottish mainland, carrying passengers, cargo and livestock. Launched by J. & G. Thomson of Clydebank (the 14th vessel built by that firm for Messrs Hutcheson), the *Clansman* replaced a three-masted ship of the same name that had been wrecked in 1869 off Sanda after only 14 years' service. The new boat incorporated some of the most attractive features of West Highland steamers of the late 19th century, including a figurehead and bowsprit, with ornamental carving at both bow and stern. She was unusual for a screw steamer in having her bridge abaft the funnel, due to the very small space between funnel and forward hold – a feature that helped to distinguish her from her near-sister ship, the *Claymore* of 1881. After nearly 40 years of uneventful but much cherished service the *Clansman* was withdrawn in 1909 and broken up the following year.

The *Claymore* of 1881 was a bigger version of the *Clansman* and generally regarded as the more handsome of the two. Working all year round in fair weather and foul, the two ships worked in tandem, the *Clansman* usually leaving Glasgow for Stornoway on Mondays and arriving back on Saturday mornings, while the *Claymore* left on Thursdays and returned on Wednesdays. Calls were made at Greenock, Oban, Tobermory and various ports on Skye and the north-west mainland before the voyage across the Minch to Stornoway. Electric lighting was installed in the *Claymore* in 1904, but her engines and boilers lasted her entire 50-year life, a remarkable achievement given their almost continuous duty.

The *Claymore* and *Clansman* usually met at Tobermory around midday every Tuesday when the *Clansman* was on her outward voyage and the *Claymore* on her way back to Glasgow. Numerous communities, big and small, depended on them for necessities, luxuries and the exchange of news and gossip, in an age that lacked the multiplication of services by sea, rail, road and air that we know today. The two steamers were an equally vital means of transporting produce to mainland markets. Among the goods carefully stowed in the hold for the voyage back to the Clyde would be bags of wool, boxes of salmon, herring and lobster, eggs, sheep and lambs. The *Claymore* and *Clansman* would also carry members of the island gentry and their servants, tourists being very much a secondary part of these boats' shipload. The final stretch of the journey home, from Oban round the Mull of Kintyre to Glasgow, would take between 11 and 12 hours, depending on the tide.

Four of the *Claymore*'s officers pose for the camera on the ship's promenade deck: (left to right) Purser Mason, Captain McAlister, Chief Steward Wallace and Chief Engineer Sorensen. Like the rest of the MacBrayne fleet the *Claymore* was crewed by Hebridean men. It speaks volumes for the skill and care of the ships' officers that accidents were so rare: daylight hours in winter were short and much intricate navigation was called for. With no radar and often no guiding lights, skippers had to rely on their local knowledge and seamanship. Many served for decades on the same ship or the same run, becoming well-kent personalities in West Highland circles – and the ships assumed a personality of their own. When the *Claymore* was broken up in 1931 at Bo'ness on the Firth of Forth, the shipbreakers received, and honoured, requests for souvenirs from all over Scotland and England.

With her yacht-like lines and clipper bow the *Chieftain* (above) was one of the most beautiful ships ever to sail to the Western Isles. At the time of her launch in 1907 from the Ailsa Company's Ayr yard she was also one of the largest built for MacBrayne. The *Chieftain* sailed on the bi-weekly Glasgow-Stornoway service alongside the much older *Clansman* (until the latter's withdrawal in 1909) and the *Claymore*, but unlike them she operated only in summer months. By 1914 traffic on the route was already in decline, and when sailings resumed after the war the *Chieftain* was deemed too costly to run. Sold in 1919 for service to Orkney and Shetland and renamed *St Margaret*, she later operated on the west coast of Canada, in the Mediterranean and to the West Indies, before being broken up in 1952. The *Chieftain* was a regular caller at Tobermory (below). In this view taken shortly before the 1914-18 war, the boat coming alongside is the *Lapwing*, a neat little passenger and cargo steamer built in 1903 for MacBrayne's Oban to Castlebay run, and used on various other routes before stranding on a rock near Oban in 1917. She was salved and taken over by Clyde Cargo Steamers Ltd, serving on the Clyde (latterly as *Cowal*) until 1931.

Though lacking the clipper bow and bowsprit of the *Clansman, Claymore* and *Chieftain*, John McCallum & Co's *Hebridean* of 1881 was scarcely less elegant: she was the first ship to have been designed by the celebrated yacht designer G.L. Watson, and attracted the same well-to-do clientele as her larger MacBrayne counterparts. Throughout the 1880s and 1890s the *Hebridean* provided the same weekly sailing for John McCallum as the *Dunara Castle* did for Martin Orme, the former leaving Glasgow on a Monday and the latter on a Thursday. After rounding the Mull of Kintyre she would sail to Oban (unlike the *Dunara Castle*, which headed for Colonsay and the west of Mull), then Coll, Tiree and a variety of ports in the Outer Hebrides, including Dunvegan in Skye, where she is pictured. Once a month in summer – usually in June, July and August – the *Hebridean* would extend her voyage to St Kilda, making her popular among tourists. In September 1885 the *Hebridean* exceptionally made a fourth trip to the remote island community, following reports that a storm had ruined their crops, threatening them with starvation during the winter. The *Hebridean* herself suffered two emergencies that same year: in March she spent four days aground in Locheport, victim of the lowest tide for 25 years; four months later she broke down off the Mull of Kintyre, whereupon the *Claymore*, also inward bound, came to her aid and towed her to Greenock. After the arrival of the larger, more up-to-date *Hebrides* in 1898, the *Hebridean* became McCallum's second steamer, usually appearing on the run only in winter. She was sold to Orkney in 1917 and sank in 1918.

In this 1920s picture of Tobermory Pier, the *Hebrides* is berthing alongside the *Claymore*. Like the *Hebridean*, her smaller predecessor, the *Hebrides* was designed by G.L. Watson and built for John McCallum & Co, whose interests ran parallel to Martin Orme & Co until their merger in 1929. In 1948, along with the rest of the McCallum Orme fleet, the *Hebrides* passed into the ownership of David MacBrayne Ltd, for whom she continued sailing until 1955, when she was broken up at Port Glasgow. Like the *Clansman* and *Claymore*, she became part of the fabric of island life.

The *Hebrides* of 1898 lies in Scalasaig Bay at Colonsay, where passengers and cargoes were transferred by ferry until the building of a pier in 1965. The cows in this picture were probably part of the cargo. For the best part of a century, until 1948, cargo services to Colonsay, Iona, Coll, Tiree, the Uists, Harris and the west coasts of Mull and Skye remained outwith the MacBrayne empire, being served almost exclusively by the ships of McCallum and Orme, whose workings were complementary to each other. The two companies' steamers were less glamorous than MacBrayne's but they maintained just as vital a service and bore the same funnel colouring – red with black top, supplemented by a black band on the red of the funnel after the two companies merged in 1929. In 1948, when MacBrayne acquired the ships and goodwill of McCallum and Orme, Colonsay was initially assigned to the Oban-based Inner Islands mail steamer, but from 1949 was added to the Islay boat's roster on the three days a week when she berthed overnight at Port Askaig.

Like Colonsay, Coll was one of the less populous islands receiving weekly calls from the *Hebrides*. When the tide was high enough she would visit the stone pier at the village of Arinagour, at the head of the only navigable bay on the more sheltered eastern side of the island. Otherwise the steamer would anchor and offload passengers and cargo into small boats. Landing by ferry at Coll continued until 1967, when a modern concrete pier was built at the entrance to the bay.

The *Islay*, the third steamer to bear the name within 25 years, was neither the prettiest of MacBrayne boats nor the luckiest. Launched in 1872 as the *Princess Louise* (left), she was one of the last ships built at the Meadowside yard of Tod & McGregor on the upper Clyde, and the first built for the Larne & Stranraer Steamboat Company. Late on delivery and slower than the contracted speed, she encountered problems from the start. After plying for 18 years on the Short Sea Route to Ireland, she was sold in 1890 to MacBrayne, who moved her bridge forward of the funnels and renamed her after the island which she was to serve from Glasgow for the following 12 years. She is pictured (centre) at Port Askaig and (bottom) on the rocks near Sheep Island, Port Ellen, where she stranded in dense fog on 15th July 1902 and became a total loss.

The *Flowerdale*, seen here at Tobermory, was one of 10 ships bought second-hand by David MacBrayne between 1887 and 1893 to bolster his services to the Western Isles. A handsome ship that had been built at Barrow in 1878 and operated on the south coast of England, she became MacBrayne's first twin-screw sea-going steamer. She was one of two steamers on his Outer Islands mail service, each of which left Oban on alternate weekday mornings. After sailing up the Sound of Mull to Tobermory, they would proceed direct to Barra and the Uists, connecting there with a steamer based at Portree. One of the *Flowerdale*'s consorts on this run was the smaller, uglier *Staffa* (below), built on the Clyde in 1861 as the *Adela* for service on the River Tagus in Portugal and later operated by various English shipowners. Purchased by MacBrayne in 1888, the *Staffa* remained in the fleet until 1909, being broken up shortly afterwards. The *Flowerdale* was lost off Lismore in 1904, but her machinery and boilers were salvaged and used in two new MacBrayne ships, the *Plover* and *Cygnet*.

The *Cygnus* was another ship built for non-Scottish waters. Launched at J. Henderson's yard at Renfrew in 1857, she traded between Weymouth and the Channel Islands and had a brief spell on the Liverpool-Isle of Man run, before being bought by David MacBrayne in 1890. After placing her initially on his Loch Fyne cargo run, MacBrayne had her rebuilt in 1892, giving her a more shapely bow and a new name, *Brigadier*. At the same time her two funnels were replaced by one aft of the paddle-box. As this picture in Oban Bay shows, she was a good-looking boat. She served on various routes, including the Outer Islands service from Portree, and was on this run when she was wrecked near Rodel, Harris, in December 1896.

The *Handa* at Blackmill Bay, Luing. For the first 10 years of her career, from 1878 to 1887, this tubby, almost comical little boat plied for Martin Orme & Co under the name *Aros Castle*, before passing into MacBrayne's hands. Only 84 feet long, with a speed of eight knots, she counts as one of the more curious vessels to have sailed in western Scottish waters, for she was short enough to negotiate the Crinan Canal but sturdy enough – just – to tackle the Minch on the Outer Islands service. She worked on a variety of routes, notably from Glasgow to Oban, Mull, Loch Sunart and Loch Leven, before being sold in 1917, after which she was abandoned at sea.

The *Cavalier* was built in 1883 for the Glasgow-Inverness service, on which she served with few exceptions for most of her career. Despite her relatively short length, necessitated by the dimensions of the locks of the Caledonian Canal, she was a handsome vessel, her nicely balanced proportions offset by two tall masts and a nicely raked funnel. Hers was a leisurely schedule, leaving Glasgow on Thursdays at 11am and Greenock Customhouse Quay around 4pm, before sailing overnight round the Mull of Kintyre and calling at western ports in Argyll during the early hours of the Friday morning. She was due at Oban around 6am, later proceeding up Loch Linnhe to Corpach and the hour-long climb up Neptune's Staircase to Banavie at the southern end of the Caledonian Canal. After berthing overnight at Banavie, she would spend Saturday negotiating the lochs and locks *en route* to Muirtown Wharf, Inverness, where she would stay until starting the return journey early on the Monday morning. The *Cavalier* had the distinction of being the first Clyde or West Highland steamer to be equipped with electric light. With the falling-off of traffic on the Glasgow-Inverness route, she was sold in 1919. After a short spell on the Orkney and Shetland run, she ended her days on the cattle run from Ireland to the Mersey, and was broken up in 1927.

A New Century

By the beginning of the 20th century the MacBrayne fleet was starting to age. So was its owner. Born in 1814, David MacBrayne had been in sole control of the company since 1878, a prosperous but somewhat reclusive Victorian businessman, working long hours with little time for activities beyond the management of his shipping company. The more David MacBrayne had expanded to remote points on the west coast, the more trade was created – and the more the company prospered. MacBrayne employed about 750 men afloat, in addition to the 700 employees on shore as agents, clerks and storemen. In 1900 his fleet consisted of 30 steamers serving 104 ports, of which 87 were north of the Mull of Kintyre.

It was at this time that MacBrayne's dominance of Hebridean transport became immortalised in the lines:

The Earth belongs unto the Lord
And all that it contains
Except the Kyles and the Western Isles
For they are all MacBrayne's

Those words, loosely based on Psalm 24, sum up the love-hate relationship between the islanders and their link with the outside world. MacBrayne's ships provided a lifeline for island communities, but like any near-monopoly, they operated by their own rules.

The new century brought new perspectives. In 1902, aged 88, David MacBrayne admitted his two sons, David Hope and Laurence, to full partnership. They had spent all their business lives in the company and now relieved their father of the day-to-day running of it. In 1905, when Laurence sold his share to his brother, a limited company was formed, with half the shares owned by David MacBrayne Snr and half by David Hope MacBrayne. On 26th January 1907, aged 92, David MacBrayne Snr died at his home at 11 Park Circus, Glasgow, leaving a company valued at £130,000.

Although several new swift steamers had been added to the fleet in the late 19th century, the majority of ships owned by MacBrayne at the start of the 20th century were second-hand. Between 1902 and 1910 that balance changed: 13 new steamers joined the fleet, a move that reflected a new lease of life in the MacBrayne operation. With the first batch of four screw steamers, the *Lapwing*, *Sheila* (below), *Plover* and *Cygnet*, the emphasis was on utility: these were intended as all-year-round boats. Gone were the handsome ornamental stems and sterns of the late 19th century. In their place came vessels with a more functional profile, some with sleeping accommodation, and all capable of providing a passenger and cargo service with maximum economy. Four subsequent newcomers, the *Clydesdale*, the *Brenda*, the second *Lochiel* and the *Dirk*, were variants on this principle.

With the *Comet*, *Scout* and *Lochinvar*, MacBrayne deserted steam power in favour of the fledgling motor engine. The fact that none of these three small ships had a funnel made them among the least noticeable, and certainly the least attractive, members of the fleet – but two of them proved their worth, lasting well over 40 years on the west coast.

The steam-driven *Chieftain*, by contrast, represented the apogee of Edwardian grandeur, beauty, comfort and expense: as times and tastes changed, she became too costly to run. The new *Mountaineer* (above at Crinan and with covered railings) and *Pioneer* proved there was still a role for the traditional paddle steamer, albeit on a more modest scale than the *Grenadier* and *Fusilier*.

With the old *Columba*, *Claymore*, *Grenadier* and other 19th century stalwarts still operating at their peak, the scene was set fair for an era of unprecedented service and stability in the Western Isles – until the Great War shattered the peace. Services were curtailed, tourist trade slumped, traffic numbers dwindled. Although, in contrast to the railway-owned steamers on the Clyde, few West Highland boats were requisitioned for war service, by 1919 David MacBrayne Ltd had lost or sold 10 of its fleet. In the next few years the *Gael* was broken up, the *Chevalier* and *Sheila* were wrecked and the *Gairlochy* and *Grenadier* destroyed by fire. As the 1920s progressed, road transport to the Highlands improved, reducing the dependence of out-of-the-way places on steamers. The tourist trade never returned to pre-war levels. An age of industrial unrest, leading to higher wages, had begun. All this impacted on the islands – and on the profit and loss account of MacBrayne's, the dominant force in island transportation. The writing was on the wall for MacBrayne's as an independent operator.

After the loss of the *Islay* in 1902, MacBrayne purchased another two-funnelled paddle steamer that soon proved her worth. The *Glendale* was the first MacBrayne acquisition of the new century, one that quickly became notable for new tonnage rather than the second-hand steamer purchases of the 1890s. She is pictured leaving Portree in July 1904, shortly after the fitting of a new set of tall, slim funnels. Built in 1875 at Govan, the *Glendale* had plied under various names and on various routes in the English and Irish Channels, the North Sea and the Thames, before joining the West Highland service. She established a good reputation on the routes on which she was used, notably the Oban-Portree-Gairloch service and the Stornoway mail run. It was while working between Glasgow and Islay that she ran aground near the Mull of Kintyre in July 1905. Neither she nor her cargo were saved, but there was no loss of life.

The *Sheila* was built in 1904 by A. & J. Inglis, Pointhouse, for MacBrayne's Stornoway service, on which she proved extremely popular and reliable over the following two decades. She was the most attractive of MacBrayne's new batch of ships, with a finely modelled hull and well-proportioned masts and funnel. She also had the distinction of being the first steamer in the fleet to be fitted with triple expansion engines. The Stornoway steamer was the hardest worked in the fleet, not only crossing the Minch twice every 24 hours, Sundays excepted, throughout the year, but often encountering the stormiest weather in the Hebrides. At 280 tons the *Sheila* was tiny by today's standards, but thanks to her sturdy build and the skill of her crew she rarely missed a voyage. Pictured at Kyle, she was wrecked at the mouth of Loch Torridon on New Year's morning 1927, while under the command of a relief skipper.

The *Plover* lies at anchor in Balmacara Bay on the north side of Loch Alsh, close to the railhead at Kyle. This was not a port of call for all MacBrayne boats, but it was the point of access from the sea for two large houses on the Balmacara estate. The *Plover*'s ferry door lies open but there is no sign of trans-shipment of goods. The port lifeboat has been lowered, and four crewmen appear to be painting the side of the hull. Of the four new screw steamers commissioned by MacBrayne's in 1903-4, the *Plover* lasted the longest – despite the fact that, when launched at Bowling in 1904, she was given the 26-year old boiler and port engine of MacBrayne's first-ever twin-screw vessel, the *Flowerdale*, which earlier that year had been wrecked off Lismore. The *Plover* proved her versatility on a variety of duties, though her staple was the Oban-Castlebay service. It was while on that service that she had the distinction of fighting off a German submarine west of Tiree in July 1918, using a single small gun at her stern. As a precaution her skipper, Captain Neil MacDougall, ordered her two lifeboats to be lowered, one of which took passengers to Rum, the other following the *Plover* overnight to Barra. The submarine submerged without further incident.

In 1934 the *Plover* was substantially altered at Ardrossan, emerging with a yellow and black funnel, an extended promenade deck aft, a hull painted half white – and a new name, *Loch Aline*. In this guise she gave excursions from Oban and took MacBrayne directors on occasional tours of the Western Isles, while continuing on island services during the winter. She was an examination vessel at Rothesay during the Second World War, after which she left the fleet, working latterly out of Dublin before being scrapped in 1951.

The *Cygnet* was another Inglis product of 1904, but lacked the well-proportioned look of her sisters. With limited passenger accommodation, a single mast and an independent cargo winch, she was designed primarily for cargo services, initially from Glasgow to Inveraray in tandem with the *Texa*, one of MacBrayne's doughty old stagers. Modified after the 1914-18 war for the mail service from Oban to Coll, Tiree, Barra and Lochboisdale, she was given a mainmast and improved accommodation, in which condition she is seen approaching Tiree. She proved increasingly unpopular, and after the arrival of a modern replacement, the *Lochearn*, in 1930, the *Cygnet* was sold for breaking up.

The *Brenda*, pictured at the North Pier, Oban, was a tubby little cargo boat, small enough to use the Crinan Canal on her journeys between Glasgow and the Firth of Lorne. Built in 1904 by Scott's of Bowling, she received a set of second-hand yacht engines that had been built in 1888, and her boiler had previously been used as an auxiliary in the *Flowerdale*. She was the last vessel on the Glasgow-Inverness run, her sailing latterly ending at Fort William. She was broken up at Troon in 1929.

Right: Of the initial batch of functional new MacBrayne steamers, the *Clydesdale* of 1905 was destined to have the longest and most varied career. Built for the bi-weekly Inverness run from Glasgow and designed on much the same lines as the *Cavalier* of 1883, she was quickly diverted to other duties after the loss of the *Glendale*. Modest, economical and a good sea boat, she became a familiar sight at many Hebridean ports, proving an ideal winter relief on services that did not require a larger ship. Pictured at Kilchoan in June 1939 while relieving on the Inner Islands mail service, the *Clydesdale* worked on a variety of runs during the 1939-45 war and was scrapped at Port Glasgow in 1953.

Below: The *Lochiel* of 1908, another Scott's of Bowling product, was the most attractive of the new breed of passenger-and-cargo steamers and the shortest-lived. Her most notable feature was a motor-operated gyromechanism, designed to reduce rolling. She served initially on the Oban-Islands mail run and later on the Portree-Outer Islands run. Requisitioned by the Admiralty in 1917 she was blown up a year later in the Bristol Channel.

Left: The Admiralty made good the loss by giving MacBrayne the *Devonia*, which had been built in 1906 for the passenger and cargo trade to Guernsey. Similar in profile to the *Clydesdale* but with an attractive overhanging stern, she was renamed *Lochiel* and put on the Glasgow-Stornoway direct cargo service. She was also used on the Glasgow-Islay weekly run: this picture shows her at Bruichladdich. The *Lochiel* proved especially useful for seasonal transportation of livestock. Laid up in 1937, she was sold back to Guernsey owners in 1938, and after the war was purchased by Greek owners.

The *Comet* of 1905 was MacBrayne's first motor vessel: there was a certain irony in the company's revival of the name that had graced the Western Isles' first commercial steam vessel. Built in London and engined by Gardner of Manchester, the *Comet* was a modest 43-ton craft with a deckhouse but no funnel. During her long career with MacBrayne's she operated on the Ballachulish-Kinlochleven run, on the Crinan Canal (where she is pictured) and latterly on the Gourock-Loch Goil run on the Clyde, by which she is best remembered. She was sold in 1947 to English owners, who employed her on short trips out of Shoreham in Sussex, where her hull was later converted for use as a houseboat.

The *Scout*, pictured in Oban Bay, was larger than the *Comet*, but despite having two masts and two promenade decks, she was no prettier. Built by Ailsa of Troon in 1907, she was placed on the Ballachulish-Kinlochleven run, suffering a premature end in 1913 when she was destroyed by fire. Her lifeboats gave further service on the *Columba* and *King George V*.

The *Lochinvar* (above) was the third and largest of MacBrayne's new motorboats. Built by Scott's of Bowling in 1908 she had a pencil-thin funnel near the stern, a crane amidships and a single mast forward of the bridge. Her passenger accommodation was adequate for the year-round Oban-Sound of Mull mail run on which she was employed for most of her MacBrayne career (in succession to the *Carabinier*). She was re-engined in 1926 and again in 1949, when she underwent an extensive refit that gave her a stouter funnel, a new crane and a covered wooden bridge. It is in this condition that she is remembered to this day, plying faithfully and unexceptionally on her daily run from Tobermory (centre) to Oban and back, criss-crossing the Sound of Mull with calls at Craignure (ferry), Lochaline, Salen and Drimnin (ferry). In 1955 she became spare and in 1959 was placed briefly on the Portree mail run, where she was not a success. Sold to English owners in 1960, she operated between Sheerness and Southend in the Thames Estuary in 1962 and 1963 under the name *Anzio I* (right), and was then laid up. In 1966 she was bought by Inverness owners for a service on the Cromarty Firth, but was wrecked on her way north near the Humber, with the loss of all her crew.

A century ago it was common practice for 200-ton paddle steamers to navigate the exposed waters of the west of Scotland, winter and summer. One such was the *Pioneer*, built by A. & J. Inglis of Pointhouse for MacBrayne's Islay run from West Loch Tarbert. When she appeared in 1905 it was considered 'modern' that her hull should be plated up to the promenade deck, instead of being cut away at the bow. The *Pioneer* served on the Islay run for 35 years, berthing on alternate nights at Port Askaig and Port Ellen, and it is at the latter port that she is pictured (top) during the Glasgow Fair, together with the *Mountaineer* on a back-up service. Each morning, six days a week in winter and summer, the *Pioneer* would leave one or other of the two Islay ports for West Loch Tarbert, calling at Gigha on her Port Ellen days and Craighouse, Jura, on her Port Askaig days. On arrival at the head of the West Loch, horse-drawn carriages would be waiting to take passengers across the isthmus to the East Loch on the Clyde, where they could catch the *Columba* back to Glasgow. The *Pioneer* would cant (centre), start loading cargoes and prepare for the carriages returning with passengers from Glasgow who had disembarked from the *Columba* at the East Loch Pier. After the outbreak of war in 1939, the *Pioneer* – in common with the rest of the MacBrayne fleet – donned wartime grey, the guise in which she is seen (bottom) at Oban in 1941 while on livestock duties. Requisitioned by the Admiralty in 1944 she returned to the Clyde and was kitted out as a research ship, before being towed to the south coast as a floating laboratory. Renamed *Harbinger* she lay at a mooring in Portland Harbour until 1958 when she was scrapped.

The *Mountaineer* of 1910, another Inglis product, was the third steamer of that name to ply under the MacBrayne flag. Like the *Pioneer*, she had a light draught and small paddle-boxes flush with the deck. Unlike her older sister, her promenade deck ended just aft of the mast, giving her a neat but old-fashioned look. Initially she appeared with boarding around the railings of her promenade deck, apparently designed to reduce passengers' exposure to the wind, but this was removed in the mid 1920s. The *Mountaineer* was a maid of all work, based at Oban except when helping out on the Islay run and relieving on MacBrayne's Loch Goil and Ardrishaig services in winter. She is pictured arriving at Crinan *circa* 1926, while the *Linnet* sits at her canal berth. She was broken up at Port Glasgow in 1938.

The *Princess Louise* of 1898 was a pretty little ship employed by her owner, Alexander Paterson, on short sea cruises from Oban in summer and livestock duties out of season. She was bought by MacBrayne's in 1934 and moved the following year to the Caledonian Canal, where she gave cruises on Loch Ness. Laid up at Ardrossan in 1939, she was later moved to Greenock and destroyed by a bombing raid in 1941 while in drydock.

A Change of Generation

The 1920s marked a turning point for David MacBrayne Ltd. The prewar boom years were but a distant memory. Fleet numbers had dwindled, services were curtailed and there were wider forces at work – inflation, industrial unrest, changing demands in the travel market – that brought the company's financial viability into question. Complaints about MacBrayne's ageing fleet mounted. The final blow was the tragic loss of the *Sheila, Chevalier* and *Grenadier* in 1927. The first two were wrecked, the last gutted by fire.

In 1928 David Hope MacBrayne, ageing son of the founder, withdrew the company's tender for the mail contract, sparking a crisis that resulted in a government-mediated rescue. The company's fleet and goodwill were taken over jointly by Coast Lines and the London Midland & Scottish Railway, under the name David MacBrayne (1928) Ltd. David Hope MacBrayne retired, bringing to an end the direct family connection with the company and its West Highland services. The new company's contract stipulated that four new ships should be built and that fares and freight charges should be lowered.

The new tonnage – squat in shape, with cruiser sterns, diesel engines and up-to-date accommodation, albeit still in two classes – was evidence of a change of generation in MacBrayne operations, a change symbolised by a new nomenclature. Starting with the *Lochness*, the first ship launched under the new contract and the last steamship built for the company, all MacBrayne ship names began with 'Loch', the second part initially being elided with the first rather than printed separately. Gradually the old favourites were withdrawn – the *Claymore* and the ancient *Glencoe* in 1931, the *Fusilier* in 1934 and the *Columba* and *Iona* in 1935. In their place came ships like the *Lochfyne* (below) and *Lochnevis* which, while noisier and less beautiful to the eye, were modern and scarcely less reliable.

The two exceptions to the 'Loch' names were the turbine steamers *King George V* and *Saint Columba*, purchased second-hand from Turbine Steamers Ltd on the Clyde, both of which retained much of the elegance of the past while setting new standards of speed and comfort for MacBrayne's. They were soon regarded with just as much affection as their predecessors on the Iona and Ardrishaig routes.

The spirit of the 1930s was captured by the company's copious advertising literature, which trumpeted the merits of its new ships to a public keen to travel and enjoy life to the full after the austerities of the 1920s and the Great Depression. Beneath a portrait of the *Lochfyne*, the 1932 summer timetable contained the following purple prose:

"Now that tourists to the Inner and Outer Hebrides have been supplied with unrivalled facilities in the way of magnificent new saloon steamers, the attention of MacBrayne's has been concentrated on supplying the perfection of comfort for increasing multitudes of people from all over the world who, whatever else they miss of the unrivalled glories of Scotland, seize the opportunity of living crowded hours of glorious and intense life on the unique day's sail from Oban to Staffa and Iona. Nothing has been spared in the equipment of the new vessel 'Lochfyne' towards ensuring the maximum of absolute ease, and the result has been the most up-to-date pleasure steamer in Scotland. The furnishings are luxurious in the artistically designed smoke-rooms and dining-rooms. On the promenade deck there is an Observation Lounge with large windows along the sides, and suitably nearby are a Soda Fountain and Ice-cream Freezer. The vessel is heated throughout by means of a hot water installation."

By drawing attention so effusively to these facilities, MacBrayne's were underlining how dated the older generation of ships had become and how eager they were to meet the rising expectations of the 1930s travelling public. Facilities such as hot running water may be taken for granted today, but they signified the height of comfort to Hebridean travellers of the 1930s. A 1937 summer brochure went so far as to describe the *Lochearn* (below, at Portree) and *Lochmor* as diminutive liners, whose "Sanitary and Heating arrangements are thoroughly up-to-date, while both Steamers are fitted with Marconi Wireless Telegraphy Installation."

MacBrayne's also addressed the growing demand for holiday cruises. In 1936 the company bought a substantial vessel from the Burns Laird Line, refurbished her and launched a series of round-trip cruises up the west coast. The *Lochgarry*, said MacBrayne's brochure, was a "roomy and seaworthy vessel...splendidly fitted and equipped for her particular service. Steam heating arrangements are of the most recent type. There are six single-berth cabins and forty-four two-berth cabins with hot and cold water. She has salt and fresh water baths, and sprays, a smoke-room with light wood panelling and furnishings with a tea, coffee, ice and cocktail bar at your elbow, sports and shelter deck, a capacious dining saloon – the ship is complete with everything that matters on a sea holiday."

With these developments the last vestiges of a Victorian-era template disappeared from Hebridean shipping services. The style of MacBrayne operations begun in the 1930s was to survive another world war and, with minor variations, endure until the late 1960s.

BAGGAGEMAN
LOC
GLA

Apart from wartime, the only occasion when MacBrayne boats were painted grey was between 1929 and 1931, when the colour was tried out on two veterans, the *Columba* and *Claymore*, and four new members of the fleet – the *Lochness*, *Lochearn*, *Lochmor* and *Lochfyne*. It was not a success. The *Lochness*, pictured soon after her debut on the Mallaig-Kyle-Stornoway run in 1929, was the first ship built for the newly constituted David MacBrayne (1928) Ltd, and the first in the fleet to bear a 'Loch' name. She proved a notable improvement on the *Sheila* in terms of comfort and capacity, had the look of a miniature liner and was a good sea boat. Replaced by the much bigger *Loch Seaforth* in 1947, she moved to the Inner Islands mail run from Oban before being sold to Greek owners in 1955.

This picture of Mallaig Harbour shows two of the four ships ordered after the re-organisation of MacBrayne services in 1928. The *Lochness*, now with black hull and enlarged funnel, is on the right, the *Lochmor* on the left. The latter entered service in 1930 on the Outer Isles mail run for which she was designed and on which she remained, with little variation, until 1964. Like the *Lochearn*, her sister, the *Lochmor* offered vastly superior accommodation to her predecessors, with comfortable cabins and more covered deck space. But with straight stems, ugly sterns and barely raked funnels, their appearance was hardly inspiring. While the new generation of boats stuck more closely to the advertised schedule than their predecessors, time-keeping was still somewhat approximate – an endearing characteristic of MacBrayne's services until the 1960s.

The *Lochearn*, the *Lochmor*'s identical sister, lies at anchor in Loch Scavaig during her first season (above). Loch Scavaig, on Skye's spectacularly scenic but sparsely populated south-western coastline, had long been one of MacBrayne's summer tourist destinations. Originally a once-a-week call on the Oban-Portree-Gairloch service, it was later turned into an excursion out of Mallaig. After being ferried ashore passengers could walk to Loch Coruisk, a rainwater loch cradled by the Cuillin mountains. The *Lochearn* was built for the Inner Islands mail service, a two-day round trip from Oban to Coll, Tiree, Barra and Lochboisdale, but she occasionally served on the *Lochmor*'s route. The two sisters were re-engined in the late 1940s, giving them a new lease of life. They were also fitted with shorter funnels. It is in this condition that the *Lochearn* is seen at Tiree (below).

The Inner and Outer Islands mail steamers regularly met at Lochboisdale in South Uist, enabling a transfer of packages. The *Lochmor* (left) and *Lochearn* were notoriously slow boats, with diesel engines that caused heavy vibration and, in later years, high-pitched screeching. Their interior fittings, including grandly named two-berth 'staterooms', nevertheless had an old-fashioned elegance, far superior to the accommodation on the boats they had replaced. Displaced by the new *Claymore* on the Inner Islands mail in 1955, the *Lochearn* succeeded the *Lochinvar* on the Sound of Mull run. In the summer of 1964 the Sound of Mull and Outer Islands mail services were axed after the inauguration of three new car ferry services to Harris/North Uist, Skye and Mull. The *Lochearn* and *Lochmor* were left to inaugurate the last of these, pretending to be car ferries for a few weeks on the new Oban-Craignure service, until the *Columba*, the third of the purpose-built ferries, was delivered. Thereafter the two ageing sisters were sold to Greek owners, leaving the Clyde for Piraeus in September 1964 with the names *Naias* and *Animoni*.

The *Lochmor* offloads cargo at Tarbert, Harris. The Outer Islands mail service was basically a thrice-weekly circumnavigation of Skye from Kyle of Lochalsh, taking in the Small Isles, the Uists, Harris and Mallaig. On Mondays the *Lochmor* was scheduled to leave Kyle at 9am for Mallaig, with intermediate stops at Glenelg and Armadale. At 1pm she would proceed to Eigg, Rum and Canna, before crossing the Minch, reaching Lochboisdale on South Uist by 9pm. She then headed north to Lochmaddy, remaining there between midnight and 5am on the Tuesday. Thereafter she would call at Rodel, Tarbert and Scalpay before heading back across the Minch, with an arrival at Kyle scheduled for shortly after 3pm. On Wednesdays and Fridays she would reverse the order, leaving Kyle at 6am for Scalpay and Tarbert, reaching Lochboisdale by 7pm. Leaving there after midnight on Thursdays and Saturdays, she would return to Mallaig and Kyle via the Small Isles.

The *Lochnevis*, built by Denny of Dumbarton in 1934, was the most versatile of the new breed of MacBrayne ships. Small and neat, with a gently raked bow, a cargo derrick for'ard and a funnel placed slightly too close to the bridge, she was designed for the Mallaig-Kyle-Portree mail run, effectively replacing the *Glencoe* of 1846, which had been withdrawn three years previously. She started and ended the war on the Wemyss Bay-Ardrishaig service, but was requisitioned in 1940 and spent three years as a minelayer. By 1946 she had returned to her original run, now with a stump mainmast (above) that became full-length in 1952 (below, at Lismore). In 1959 she was transferred to Oban for summer cruising – a role to which she was well suited, as she had ample deck space and a foredeck which allowed passengers to go right up to the bow. In winter she performed relief work on the Islay, Ardrishaig and Sound of Mull mail runs. In the late 1960s the *Lochnevis* provided additional capacity on the Islay service at summer weekends, returning to Oban from Colonsay on Monday evenings for midweek excursions to Fort William and the Six Lochs. She was sold to Dutch owners in 1970 and broken up in 1974.

The *Lochiel*, the third MacBrayne boat to bear that name, was built by Denny of Dumbarton in 1939 for the Islay run. She continued the basic schedule set by her predecessor, the *Pioneer*, operating alternately to Port Ellen and Port Askaig, where she is pictured (above) sometime before 1953, when she was fitted with a mainmast. Again like the *Pioneer*, the *Lochiel* called at Craighouse, Jura (below), on the days of her call at Port Askaig, but from 1949 those sailings were extended to include Colonsay. Apart from her first summer, when she was based at Oban while the pier at West Loch Tarbert was being dredged, the *Lochiel* spent her entire MacBrayne career on the Islay run, stopping only for her brief annual overhaul in Greenock. The build-up of traffic on the Islay run in the 1960s led to the introduction of a supplementary service in summer, undertaken by the *Lochnevis*, but with the start of Western Ferries' stern-loading ferry service from Kennacraig in April 1968, it became obvious that the two older boats were ill equipped to compete. The *Lochiel* was sold in 1970 for use as a ferry between Fleetwood and Douglas, Isle of Man, for which she was renamed *Norwest Laird*. The venture was not successful, and she later became a floating restaurant at Bristol, with the name *Lochiel* restored. She was scrapped in 1995.

Unlike her near-contemporaries the *Lochfyne* had two funnels (the forward one a dummy) and was a passenger-only boat. She had one other distinction: she was the first British passenger vessel to be directly powered by diesel-electric engines. Thanks to the noise and vibration they generated, together with her stiff appearance, she remained an under-appreciated member of the fleet. The *Lochfyne* was initially employed on the Iona and Staffa excursion in summer and the Ardrishaig mail service on the Clyde in winter, in which combination she effectively replaced the *Grenadier*. After the arrival of the *King George V* at Oban in 1936 her summer employment was focused on the service to Fort William, where she is pictured. During the Second World War the *Lochfyne* carried out the Ardrishaig service from Wemyss Bay, and it was on that route (from Gourock) that she spent her last 11 years before being withdrawn in September 1969. Thereafter she spent some time at Faslane in the Gareloch, providing electric power for the ship-breaking yard there. She was broken up at Dalmuir in 1974.

The *Saint Columba* at speed. In 1935 MacBrayne's bought two Clyde turbine steamers from Turbine Steamers Ltd. One was the *King George V*, a Denny product of 1926, which was transferred in unaltered condition (except funnel colouring) to the Iona excursion and became an Oban institution for the next 40 years. The other was the *Queen Alexandra* of 1912, a ship with a distinguished war record and an outstanding turn of speed. She underwent a radical remodelling, emerging for the 1936 season with three funnels (the aft one a dummy) and a new name, *Saint Columba* – signifying that while no ship could ever match the legendary *Columba* on the Glasgow-Ardrishaig mail service, she could at least prove a worthy successor. In 1937 the *Saint Columba* became the first Clyde steamer to be converted from coal to oil burning. After spending the war years as an accommodation ship in Greenock, she resumed her sailings in 1947 (from Gourock), and by the time of her withdrawal in 1958, she was widely recognised as the most handsome steamer on the Clyde. She was broken up at Port Glasgow.

After the withdrawal of the old *Claymore* in 1931, MacBrayne's needed a ship to satisfy the summer tourist trade on the Glasgow-west coast route. The *City of London*, a passenger and cargo steamer that had been engaged on Britain's east coast for the previous 40 years, was even older than the *Claymore*, and not nearly as good-looking, but she had newer boilers. Refitted and renamed *Lochbroom*, she left Glasgow every 10 days for Oban and the north, sometimes venturing as far as Loch Clash in Sutherland. Pictured at Badentarbet, north of Ullapool, she was broken up in 1937.

Among the cruises undertaken by MacBrayne steamers out of Oban was a trip up Loch Sunart, one of the most scenic lochs on the west coast. In the right tidal conditions it included a spectacularly narrow passage between Glenborrodale on the mainland (left) and the island of Risga (right), viewed here from the bow of the 1910 *Mountaineer*.

The ship closest to the pier at Tobermory (above) is the *Lochgarry*, with the *Mountaineer* on the outside and the *Lochinvar* sandwiched in between. The *Lochgarry* was bought from the Burns Laird Line in 1937 to take the *Lochbroom*'s place on the West Highland summer cruise roster. Launched in 1898 as the *Vulture* and later renamed *Lairdsrock*, she had spent her early career on the Ardrossan-Belfast night service. Extensively remodelled by MacBrayne, the *Lochgarry* cut a fine profile and was at that time the largest ship to have sailed under the MacBrayne flag. Requisitioned in 1940, she took part in the evacuation at Dunkirk and later served as a transport between Scotland and Iceland. It was while on this run that she foundered off Rathlin Island in January 1942, with the loss of 23 of her crew. In the photograph (below) of members of the *Lochgarry*'s crew, John MacCallum, her Tiree-born Second Officer, stands in the centre. As the *King George V*'s long-serving Mate in the post-war era, MacCallum became one of the most popular and well-known officers in the MacBrayne fleet.

After the War

During the 1939-45 war, services to the Western Isles were cut to essentials and the fleet was painted grey. The *King George V* headed for the English Channel, where she distinguished herself at the Dunkirk and Rotterdam evacuations. The *Saint Columba* remained on the Clyde as a stationary accommodation ship in Greenock. Mail services to Ardrishaig, Islay, the Inner and Outer Isles and Stornoway were maintained by the ships introduced to the fleet since 1928. There may have been deprivation, late running and variable standards of service, but apart from the *Lochgarry*, which was sunk off Ireland, the fleet suffered no wartime losses.

It was not until 1947 that services returned to something resembling pre-war normality, and in 1948 a further step-change in West Highland services took place. Under the new Labour Government's Transport Act, the London Midland & Scottish Railway – half-owner of MacBrayne – was nationalised and its shareholding in the company transferred to the new British Transport Commission, later known as British Railways. At the same time MacBrayne took over McCallum Orme & Co, whose ships had offered complementary sailings for the best part of a century. MacBrayne now had a virtual monopoly over services to the Western Isles.

A fleet of 18 vessels could celebrate the MacBrayne centenary in 1951, but its composition was in flux. Five of those ships dated from before the First World War and would soon be sold without replacement. Loss-making cargo services faced drastic surgery in the face of the increasing use of road transport. In 1951 the west mainland service north of Kyle of Lochalsh was discontinued, bringing to an end historic MacBrayne calls at Gairloch, Aultbea, Lochinver and Loch Clash. Scorraig on the east side of Little Loch Broom, which had no access road, was reprieved pending the provision of a local ferry service. Bit by bit calls at other small communities, such as Salen (Loch Sunart) and the west coast of Mull, were axed.

But the three surviving cargo runs from Glasgow – to Islay, the Outer Isles and Stornoway – saw a steady rise in total carryings and profits after the replacement of old tonnage by three new vessels, the *Lochdunvegan*, *Loch Carron* (right, at Lochmaddy) and *Loch Ard*. Thanks to rationalisation of mail services, small communities such as Applecross, Lismore and Kilchoan were given dedicated services by small craft. Since 1947 Stornoway had been enjoying the services of an impressive new mail boat, the *Loch Seaforth*. In 1955 another new boat, the *Claymore*, was launched at Denny's of Dumbarton (below), raising standards of speed and comfort on the Inner Islands mail run. At the same time MacBrayne buses were proliferating in the Highlands and Islands, creating an integrated network of land and sea transportation.

Despite such obvious traces of post-war modernisation, an old-world innocence could still be detected in services to the Western Isles in the 1950s. The arrival of the MacBrayne boat was just as much a focal point of island life as it had been for the previous hundred years: it was still called the 'steamer', even though by the end of the decade there was only one steam-driven ship left, the *King George V*. MacBrayne's time-keeping remained endearingly approximate, as if the demands of the outside world did not really apply to the Hebrides. The division of accommodation into First and Third Class was an enduring anachronism. On the Islay, Inner Islands and Outer Islands runs, calls were still being made at places where there was no pier, necessitating the precarious transfer of passengers and cargo by small ferryboat from ship to shore.

The ships were still crewed by Hebridean men who spent their lives serving the island communities. Some gave their lives in that service, such as the two Craignure ferrymen, George Clyne and James Bennet, who drowned while trying to secure the ferryboat *Craignure* during a gale on 26th July 1957 (below, ferryboats at Craignure). Others became kenspeckle figures, their seamanship and local knowledge providing a guarantee of reliability in fair weather and foul. One such was Captain Duncan Robertson, who retired in May 1949 after 32 years' service – 27 of them as Master on the Outer Isles mail service, crossing the Minch in all weathers without ever having an accident. When asked what had been his worst experience in all those years, he replied "Income Tax".

In the 1950s, when you stepped across the gangway of a MacBrayne steamer, with its red-and-black funnel gleaming in the sun and its Gaelic-speaking crew resplendent in pill-box hats, you felt as if you were taking a step back from the hurly-burly of modern life. All that was to change in the 1960s with the arrival of purpose-built car ferries.

Plans to upgrade the Stornoway service had been laid before the war but it was 1945 before a replacement for the *Lochness* was ordered and 1947 before the *Loch Seaforth* was launched at Denny's yard in Dumbarton on the Clyde. Like the *Lochness* she had a high forecastle, a shade deck and cruiser stern, but all her cargo accommodation was forward of the bridge and her dumpy red-and-black funnel was set well back: the deep black top was narrowed in 1966 but reverted to deep in 1972. She would leave Mallaig at 12.15pm every day except Sundays for Armadale (top), Kyle (centre) and Stornoway, setting off again from the Lewis port at 11.45pm (12.15am on Mondays). In 1949 she became the first MacBrayne boat to be fitted with radar, but it didn't stop her running aground on several notable occasions – the last of which was to be her undoing. Transferred to Oban in 1972, she ran aground in Gunna Sound, between Coll and Tiree, in March 1973. After being towed to Tiree Pier she sank and had to be beached. Patched and refloated (bottom) she was taken to Troon for scrapping: an ignominious end for a fine ship.

The *Claymore* revived the name of one of her most distinguished MacBrayne predecessors. Built by Denny of Dumbarton in 1955, she incorporated such traditional features as a cargo-handling derrick and a Highlander insignia on her bow, while representing modernity in her navigation aids, the comfort of her accommodation and the styling of her tripod foremast and domed funnel. She spent most of her Hebridean career on the Inner Isles mail run, leaving Oban on Mondays, Wednesdays and Fridays at 7am for Tobermory, Coll, Tiree (top), Castlebay and Lochboisdale – returning across the Minch during the night to arrive back at Oban in the forenoon. On Tuesday, Thursday and Saturday afternoons in summer she sometimes gave cruises to Fort William (centre) and Colonsay. She was also used as a relief boat on the Stornoway run. Within a decade the *Claymore* was starting to look old-fashioned. Purpose-built car ferries had been introduced to the Clyde in 1954, and after the commissioning of the *Clansman*, *Columba* and *Hebrides* in 1964, vehicle traffic to and from the Western Isles began to multiply. By the mid 1970s, barely 20 years after entering service, the *Claymore* was redundant. Sold to Greece, she was extensively remodelled and became well known as the *City of Hydra* (bottom), cruising in the Aegean Sea.

Kilchoan, also known as Mingary, on the Ardnamurchan Peninsula was for many years served by the Inner Isles mail steamer, which sailed thrice-weekly from Oban and Tobermory to Coll, Tiree, Barra and South Uist. Under the terms of the 1947 mail contract MacBrayne agreed to operate a new service between Kilchoan and Tobermory, linking with the Sound of Mull steamer. It was not until April 1949 that the *Lochbuie*, a converted RAF rescue boat, inaugurated the run, on which she continued until 1968. She is pictured arriving at Kilchoan Pier, with the mountains of Mull in the background.

MacBrayne's bought the hospital launch *Galen* in 1946, renamed her *Lochnell* and placed her on a new twice-daily return service between Oban and Lismore. Built on the Clyde in 1941, she was a neat little craft with a small cabin, a transom stern and a certificate for 25 passengers in summer, 12 in winter. Initially she appeared with a black hull, which later went through varying shades of blue. In 1965 she moved to the Toscaig run from Kyle of Lochalsh, and in 1968 to the Tobermory-Kilchoan run. Sold in 1981, she is still in use as a private launch.

Passengers wait to board the *Loch Arkaig* at Mallaig for a trip to the Small Isles. Built in 1942 as a wooden inshore minesweeper, the *Loch Arkaig* joined the MacBrayne fleet in 1959. After being re-engined and given a new lightweight metal superstructure she was placed on the Mallaig-Portree run, on which she proved to be a handy little boat. In 1964 she added the Small Isles to her duties, serving on that run exclusively from 1975 until 1979, when she sank in Mallaig Harbour. She was considered not worth repairing.

The *Loch Eynort*, pictured (above) at Raasay Pier, was another member of MacBrayne's postwar fleet that had seen useful service elsewhere before being purchased for service on the west of Scotland. As the *Valonia* she had worked as a pilot boat in Ireland from 1947 until 1961. Renamed *Loch Eynort*, she took up the Kyle-Portree run in 1962, while also giving occasional cruises. Taken off the Skye service in 1965, she did occasional relief duties, and was used for a passenger-only service between Mallaig and Armadale in 1970, memorably acting as a tender to the *King George V* during the latter's charter that year by the Highlands and Islands Development Board (right). She was sold to an English buyer in 1971.

By the 1950s the *King George V* was an Oban institution, undertaking the 'Sacred Isle Cruise' to Iona every day except Sundays between late May and mid September. On five days a week she also stopped at Staffa, until ferry landings there were halted in 1967 after a rock fall: thereafter the steamer merely slowed down as she passed Fingal's Cave. Built by Denny of Dumbarton in 1926 for Turbine Steamers Ltd's excursion sailings to Campbeltown and Inveraray, the *King George V* had the distinction of being the first Clyde steamer to have an enclosed shelter deck. She became MacBrayne's Iona steamer in 1936 (top), donned wartime grey in 1939 (bottom) and served at the Dunkirk evacuation in 1940, her distinguished exploits there being later commemorated by a plaque on board (inset). After the war she undertook the Ardrishaig mail service for a year in place of the *Saint Columba*, which remained in Admiralty hands until late in 1946. The *King George V* resumed her Iona duties the following summer and remained on the route until 1974, occasionally relieving on the Clyde in early and late season. Every winter until the *Saint Columba's* withdrawal in 1958, the two steamers would lie alongside each other in Greenock's East India Harbour, their five red-and-black funnels making an unforgettable sight.

As the 1960s drew to a close, fuel prices began to rocket and MacBrayne's started developing the overland route to Iona via Craignure and Fionnphort, raising questions over the *King George V*'s future. Beautifully kept as she was by her crew, many of them islanders who returned to her summer after summer, the ageing steamer began to look like an expensive anachronism. She was withdrawn after the 1974 summer season, two years short of her 50th birthday. Latterly she was no flier – unlike her Clyde counterparts, she rarely exceeded 15 knots – but few steamers commanded such affection among the travelling public. In May 1970 the *King George V* undertook two unusual charters – a day cruise from Ayr to Bangor in Northern Ireland for the Coastal Cruising Association, and a week-long excursion programme for the Highlands and Islands Development Board, taking her north of Ardnamurchan Point for the only time in her career. Despite atrocious weather and several cancelled sailings, it was enjoyed by a group of intrepid steamer enthusiasts (right), who were able to buy £5 tickets for the entire week. In 1973, after David MacBrayne Ltd and the Caledonian Steam Packet Company were merged to create Caledonian MacBrayne Ltd, the *King George V* was given lions on her funnels (below, at Tobermory) in accordance with the new company's colour scheme – an addition that did little for her appearance. After her withdrawal, she was bought by a consortium hoping to turn her into a floating restaurant in South Wales. Before that could be realised, she was gutted by fire in dry dock at Cardiff and left to disintegrate on a sandbank in the Bristol Channel, a sad end for one of the finest steamers to grace the Western Isles.

Few MacBrayne boats of the early post-war era had a more varied past than the *Robina*. A twin-screw steamer of old-fashioned design, she was built in 1914 for excursion sailings in Morecambe Bay, and later operated out of Blackpool, Belfast and Bristol Channel ports, before arriving in the Clyde as a tender during the Second World War. MacBrayne's chartered her in 1946, initially for summer excursions out of Oban and later for the Islay run. In 1947 she replaced MacBrayne's pioneer motor boat, the *Comet*, on the run from Gourock to Lochgoilhead, where she is pictured. Traffic was poorer than expected and she was laid up at Greenock. After leaving the Clyde in 1948, she worked in the Channel Islands and the Solent, and was broken up in 1958.

The *Loch Toscaig* was another of MacBrayne's post-war purchases with an exotic past – as a fishing boat. Built in 1945, she came into the Hebridean fleet in 1956, her fish-holds converted into a cargo hold and her crew quarters into passenger accommodation. She provided a new service between Toscaig (left) and Kyle of Lochalsh, thereby relieving the Stornoway mail boat of calls at Applecross. From the mid 1960s to the mid 1970s she was the Lismore boat (right). Sold in 1975, she was used for fishing trips out of Gourock, but became a wreck after being blown off her moorings in 1978.

The improvement of transport links to the Highlands and Islands after the Second World War led to a rapid dwindling of traffic by sea from Glasgow. One by one the old cargo boats were disposed of, including the *Lochdunvegan*. Built in 1891 and used by a succession of owners on cargo routes between Scotland and Ireland, she came under the MacBrayne flag in 1928 and worked on the Stornoway, Islay and Fort William cargo runs from Glasgow. She was scrapped in 1948.

Another older-generation MacBrayne cargo ship to face the axe early in the post-war era was the *Lochgorm*, pictured (right) in 1950 in the Kingston Dock, Glasgow, with the *Loch Frisa*. The *Lochgorm* was built in 1896 as the *Lily* (later *Lairdspool*) for the Laird Line and did not enter MacBrayne service until 1937. In 1947 her masts were severely truncated, to the detriment of her appearance. She was broken up in 1951. The *Loch Frisa* (left), named after the largest inland loch on Mull, was built in Canada in 1946 as the *Ottawa Maycliff*. After initially sailing for Dutch owners she was bought by MacBrayne in 1949 and used on various cargo services until 1963, when she was sold to Greece.

Two other additions to MacBrayne's post-war cargo fleet were the *Lochdunvegan* and the *Loch Broom* – both, like the *Loch Frisa*, purchased second-hand. The *Loch Broom*, pictured at Bruichladdich on Islay, had been built at the end of the war as a patrol vessel for the Far East, with the name *Empire Maysong*. She came into the MacBrayne fleet in 1947 and was redesigned, the bridge being moved from near the bow to the stern. She was used mostly on the Glasgow-Islay run and for sheep-carrying duty based at Oban. She was sold in 1971.

The *Lochdunvegan*, built in Sweden in 1946 as the *Ornen*, entered MacBrayne's service in 1950 on the run from Glasgow to Stornoway, where she is pictured late in her Hebridean career ahead of the car ferry *Iona*. Fitted with refrigerating apparatus for the Lewis fish trade, she also undertook vehicle-carrying sailings from Oban to Tiree and from Uig to Tarbert, Harris. The *Lochdunvegan* was distinctive for her short, elliptical superstructure, giving the impression of a stern-heavy ship with a high-lying bow. She became surplus to requirements in 1973 and was sold abroad.

MacBrayne's fleet of cargo ships continued to serve the islands until October 1975, with passenger accommodation in most cases limited to four berths. The last ship to be built for this purpose was the *Loch Ard*, a product of Fergusons of Port Glasgow in 1955. Pictured in the Clyde early in her career, she took over the old *Hebrides'* fortnightly Outer Isles run from Glasgow, moving in 1964 to the Islay run. She was sold to Greek owners in 1971 and sank in the Mediterranean in 1984.

The last ship to operate MacBrayne's cargo service to the isles was the *Loch Carron*, seen here in 1969 beneath the new Kingston Bridge on the Clyde at Glasgow. Purpose-built in 1951, she had a pleasing modern profile and was the first boat in the fleet to be fitted with hydraulic machinery. She was sold to Cypriot owners in 1977.

Car Ferry Revolution

By the late 1950s the UK was enjoying levels of prosperity that had been unthinkable in the immediate aftermath of the Second World War. Thanks to educational, social and technological advances, car ownership and tourism came within reach of a wide swathe of British society. The burgeoning middle classes had higher disposable income, more leisure time and wider opportunities to enjoy it. These developments, while slow to reach the Western Isles, influenced the way transport policy evolved.

During the 1950s car ferries had begun to revolutionise Clyde and cross-channel services, but Hebridean life continued at its own leisurely pace – a remnant of old ways in a world that was fast changing. Transfers from ship to shore at Coll (left), Colonsay, Eigg and Rum continued to be by small ferry. Elsewhere cars were still being loaded and unloaded individually by ship's derrick or crane – a tortuous, time-consuming operation that could not cope with heavy vehicles (right). It was not until 1964, with the arrival of purpose-built car ferries, that the evolution of transportation in the Western Isles took its next step, altering routes that in basic form had changed little since the First World War.

The first indication of a modern system of vehicle transportation in the islands came in 1960, when MacBrayne announced plans for three car ferries. The intention was to shorten sea routes and increase the use of roads, focusing on new services from Uig (Skye) to Lochmaddy (North Uist) and Tarbert (Harris), from Mallaig to Armadale (Skye) and from Oban to Craignure (Mull) and Lochaline (Morvern). The irony was that most of the roads to the mainland terminals still had long single-width stretches with passing places, and the condition of island roads can only be imagined. MacBrayne's had no control over this.

David MacBrayne Ltd had no capital of its own to invest in new tonnage. Given the meagre subsidy it was receiving at the time, the company was unable to finance the three new ships – never mind the building or upgrading of piers to accommodate them. And so a new funding mechanism was put in place whereby the Secretary of State for Scotland owned the ships and MacBrayne operated them. This explains why, at least to begin with, the three ferries' port of registry was Leith rather than Glasgow. It also explains the three ferries' design – like mini-liners with sleeping cabins, though none was to work on a route of more than two and a half hours' duration. In the Cold War atmosphere prevailing in the early 1960s, the ferries had to be able to double as floating nuclear fallout shelters for civil servants from St Andrew's House in Edinburgh, should the need arise.

MacBrayne's naively believed that the development of new traffic and the rationalisation of services would in time reduce the need for subsidy on sea routes to the islands. The opposite proved to be the case. Although MacBrayne's got rid of the loss-making Sound of Mull and Outer Islands mail runs, it effectively replaced two unsophisticated ships (the *Lochearn* and *Lochmor*) with three modern car ferries, plus the *Loch Eynort* on the rump of its Skye service from Kyle to Raasay and Portree. Operating profit dropped from £231,710 in 1963, the year before the new ferries were introduced, to £99,640 in 1964, with the Secretary of State for Scotland paying an increased subsidy of £366,000 compared to £220,000 in 1963.

If this was what happened when loss-makers were replaced, where was the incentive to replace ships that were profitable, such as the *Loch Seaforth* and *Claymore*? In 1964 the latter was only nine years old but already as obsolete as the *Lochearn* and *Lochmor*, except on a grander scale. Like the *Lochiel* and *Lochnevis* at Islay, the *Claymore* struggled to cope with increased traffic to Coll, Tiree and Barra. By the end of the decade, it became obvious that new tonnage was needed – and more subsidy.

To their early users the three new car ferries – the *Hebrides*, *Clansman* and *Columba* – were indeed revolutionary. They sent an unequivocal message to the outside world: travel to the Western Isles was quick, easy and affordable. But by generating a rapid increase in traffic they soon demonstrated their inadequacy – and that of the old-fashioned terminals they were using. The loading and unloading of vehicles was carried out by hydraulic lift, from the sides of which ramps were lowered onto the pierside. The process took account of the variable state of the tide and was faster than by crane, but with roll-on/roll-off ferries already being introduced elsewhere, it looked cumbersome and slow. After only nine seasons the *Columba* had to quit Oban and take up secondary routes. At the same age the *Clansman* underwent an expensive conversion, emerging as a drive-through roll-on/roll-off ferry. The *Hebrides* (below, at Uig) soldiered on until 1985.

By the end of the 1960s the cycle of change was gathering speed. A new organisation, the Scottish Transport Group (STG), assumed control of government-subsidised shipping interests in the Clyde and Western Isles, injecting fresh investment into the transport network and making possible the transfer of ships from one area to the other. Having been outmanoeuvred by the privately owned Western Ferries on the Islay run, the STG went through a tortuous process of trying to re-establish MacBrayne's presence there. At Skye, too, the new organisation initially struggled to keep up with the new realities, but by 1971 two large end-loading ferries were operating on the short crossing from Kyle to Kyleakin, replacing older ferries that had been swamped by the build-up of traffic.

That left the crossing to Lewis. After the replacement of the *Loch Seaforth* on the traditional Mallaig-Kyle-Stornoway run in 1970, it took three years and three different ferries before a stable solution was found – a new service from Ullapool, the first roll-on/roll-off facility in the MacBrayne empire.

In 1973 STG's shipping interests were transferred to a new organisation, Caledonian MacBrayne Ltd (known as CalMac), whose corporate identity was emblazoned on funnels in the shape of a yellow disc with red lion. The modern era had begun.

MacBrayne's had been slow to wake up to the post-war boom in car ownership and its implications for tourism and mobility. The old fleet of ships was poorly equipped to cope. While the arrival of three new car ferries in 1964 revolutionised sea transport to Mull, Skye and Harris, services to other islands – notably Islay, Jura, Gigha, Colonsay, Coll, Tiree and Barra – remained in the dark ages until the early 1970s. Traffic on the Islay route built up throughout the 1960s and the *Lochiel*, which had served faithfully on the run since 1940, proved increasingly inadequate. Although her passenger accommodation was comfortable, with settees in her forward observation lounge and plentiful deck space, she could carry only a handful of cars, strapped to the open deck forward of her bridge. She was operating from the same terminal in shallow waters at the head of West Loch Tarbert that Islay mail boats had used for more than a century. Cars had to be manhandled onto the deck using slings and cargo derricks, a primitive and time-consuming manoeuvre that made for colourful pierside scenes such as these. Once underway, it still took 20 minutes for the boat to sail down the loch and reach the open sea. Nevertheless, for many holidaymakers a leisurely voyage to Islay on the *Lochiel* represented the final step on the road to paradise.

MacBrayne's three new car ferries were all built by Hall Russell of Aberdeen, where the *Hebrides* (left) and the *Clansman* are pictured taking shape early in 1964. The *Hebrides* was the first of the ferries to appear: she made a special voyage up the Clyde to Glasgow in early April to advertise herself to public and press, before inaugurating the new triangle service linking Uig with Lochmaddy and Tarbert, Harris, on 15th April 1964. For islanders in the 1960s it was the height of modernity to drive onto a ferry. A hydraulic lift fitted with turntables lowered the cars to a special deck where they were 'garaged' for the sea crossing. In the 1970s and 1980s the proliferation of drive-through ferries with bow and stern ramps rendered the pioneering MacBrayne car ferries obsolete. In 1985 the *Hebrides* was sold to Torbay Seaways for service between Torquay and the Channel Islands, under the name *Devoniun*. She was later sold to Greek owners and renamed *Illyria*.

In June 1964 the *Clansman* took up her summer-only service on the 20-minute crossing from Mallaig to Armadale. From 1967 her schedule included an overnight trip on Fridays to Lochboisdale, later extended in 1971-2 to include Castlebay on a thrice-weekly basis. For such purposes her 50 sleeping berths came in handy. Like her two sisters, the *Clansman* could comfortably carry 600 passengers and 50 cars, the latter stored in a garage-type area on the main deck. In 1969 she became the first MacBrayne boat to circumnavigate Britain, berthing in London at Tower Pier for 10 days as part of a Highlands and Islands Development Board promotion. The following year her funnel was temporarily painted yellow and black while she was serving on the Gourock-Dunoon run on the Clyde, under charter to the Caledonian Steam Packet Company.

In 1972, less than 10 years after entering service, the *Clansman* was sent to Troon for a rebuild that took nine months. Her hull was lengthened by 36 feet forward of her superstructure, which was raised to give more headroom in the car deck. Her lift was removed, and bow and stern doors were installed to enable drive-through operation. She was given two new masts, twin rudders and a more powerful bow-thrust, and in June 1973 took up service on the Ullapool-Stornoway run.

The *Clansman*'s rebuild was not the hoped-for success. She looked ungainly, as if all her superstructure had been dumped on the aft end of the hull. Her increased length led to a loss in speed and made her unwieldy in heavy seas. Amid mounting complaints she was moved to other routes, latterly serving on the Ardrossan-Brodick run on the Clyde. After breaking down in March 1984 the *Clansman* spent the summer languishing in dock at Greenock, and was sold to English owners for a proposed new service linking Devon and the Channel Islands. When this did not materialise, she was sold to Malta, where she was renamed *Tamira* and later *Al Hussein*. In 1986 she moved to the Gulf of Aqaba, sailing under the name *Al Rasheed* but still recognisable by the unfortunate shape she had assumed in 1973.

The last of the newcomers was the *Columba*, which entered service on 30th July 1964 between Oban and a new pier at Craignure (above), with an onward extension of the run (later dropped) across the Sound of Mull to Lochaline. It was not long before the *Columba*'s hydraulic lift starting looking as old-fashioned as the traditional derrick on the *Lochearn*, the ship she had replaced. Displaced from the Mull service by the mid 1970s, she moved to a variety of other duties, including the Coll, Tiree and Colonsay runs, and cruises to Iona after the *King George V*'s withdrawal in 1974. The *Columba* also undertook special sailings to St Kilda in 1978 and 1980 – the first Hebridean service boat to land passengers there since the island's evacuation in 1930.

In 1988 the *Columba* was purchased by a specialist cruise operator and given a new lease of life and a new name – *Hebridean Princess*. Extensively rebuilt by George Prior of Great Yarmouth, with luxury accommodation for 49 passengers serviced by a crew of 38, she began revisiting most of her MacBrayne haunts and many new ones too. In July 2006 she was chartered by Queen Elizabeth for a summer holiday in the Hebrides, the first time the British monarch and her family had undertaken such a sail since the 'retirement' of the Royal Yacht *Britannia* in December 1997. The *Hebridean Princess* is pictured in May 2009 passing beneath the Skye Bridge.

The ferry that inaugurated the Ullapool-Stornoway run in March 1973 was the *Iona*, seen here at Ullapool. The first of a second generation of MacBrayne car ferries, she was also the first drive-through ferry in the fleet – and the first with retractable stabilisers. There were other novelties: a bow visor and a low, open stern with ramp. But the old hydraulic lift and side-ramps were also fitted, a sign of the slow progress being made in the conversion of Hebridean piers to drive-on/drive-off usage. Launched at Ailsa, Troon, in January 1970, the *Iona* was originally intended for the Islay run, but began her career sailing between Gourock and Dunoon on the Clyde. Her distinguishing features were her tiny funnel (initially painted yellow and black), her impressive speed – 17.51 knots on trial – and the modesty of her passenger accommodation. In April 1972, with funnel now painted red, she moved to the Western Isles, and over the following 25 years visited every pier on the CalMac roster – the only ferry to have achieved this feat. In 1975 she underwent a transformation: the little funnel was removed, her parallel exhausts were extended by six feet and painted in CalMac colours, and a deckhouse was added to her upper deck. Latterly known by the nickname "Ten-n-a", she was sold in 1997 for service on the Pentland Firth and renamed *Pentalina B*, but occasionally returned to her old routes on charter to CalMac. She left UK waters in January 2010, after being purchased by a company in the Cape Verde Islands.

The *Suilven*, originally ordered by a Norwegian ferry operator, was still on the stocks at her builders near Oslo when she was acquired by CalMac in 1974. She was not much faster than the *Clansman*, but with room for 120 cars she had greater capacity – a crucial factor on the Ullapool-Stornoway run, which was attracting large numbers of heavy vehicles. She undertook two return sailings daily in summer, one in winter (increased to two from 1979), with a scheduled journey time of three and a half hours, and a half-hour turn-round – berthing bow-in at Stornoway, stern-in at Ullapool. Like several of her predecessors in the fleet, she became a victim of her own success. When the bigger, faster *Isle of Lewis* joined the fleet in July 1995, the *Suilven* was sold to New Zealand where, on passage between the North and South Islands, she faced even fiercer seas than the Minch. In 2004 she was sold to a shipping company in Fiji.

The car ferry revolution was late in coming to Islay, and when it finally did, in April 1968, it was ushered in not by MacBrayne's but Western Ferries Ltd. This unsubsidised company was backed by commercial interests on Islay and Jura who wanted a cheap, frequent, no-frills service – exactly what the stern-loading *Sound of Islay* (above) supplied from a specially constructed terminal at Kennacraig near the mouth of West Loch Tarbert. Such was her success that a larger, Norwegian-built drive-through ferry, the *Sound of Jura* (below) replaced her in 1969, and a small landing craft was acquired for the short crossing from Port Askaig to Feolin in Jura. By 1971 Western Ferries seemed to be winning the battle with MacBrayne's, but three years later CalMac hit back with a bigger subsidy, a purpose-built boat (the *Pioneer*) and converted terminals at West Loch Tarbert and Port Ellen. Western Ferries wound down its Islay operations in the late 1970s.

MacBrayne's initial response to Western Ferries was to order its own roll-on roll-off ferry (the *Iona*) – only to find Argyll County Council refusing to support the building of a new terminal. The formation of the Scottish Transport Group in 1969, merging the Caledonian Steam Packet Company's Clyde operations with MacBrayne's in the Western Isles, paved the way for an interim solution: the *Iona* was switched to the Clyde, and the Clyde's first purpose-built car ferry, the *Arran* of 1953, was moved round to Islay, where she could use existing terminals. With her funnel repainted red with black top, the *Arran* is seen at the old MacBrayne pier at the head of West Loch Tarbert (above) shortly after taking up the Islay run in January 1970. After three years she was given a substantial makeover, involving the removal of her lift and aft superstructure and the introduction of a stern ramp. The new-look *Arran* survived one more year on the Islay run, for which her 30-car capacity had become inadequate, before being redeployed elsewhere, including sailings from Oban to Craignure and Lochaline (below). The *Arran* ended her CalMac career in 1979 on the Small Isles run. After lying idle on the Clyde for two years, she was towed to Dublin in 1981 for use as a floating restaurant, but this was short-lived and she moved in 1986 to Manchester, where a similar venture was planned. She was broken up in 1993.

The *Glen Sannox*, pictured at Port Askaig, was another former side-loading Clyde ferry that found new life in the Western Isles. Built at Troon in 1957 for the Arran service she joined the West Highland fleet in 1974, initially on the Oban-Craignure run. She subsequently served Coll, Tiree, Colonsay and Islay. She also acted as a summer cruise steamer on the Clyde, before being withdrawn in 1989. The *Glen Sannox* is remembered as one of the most popular ferries to serve the islands, not least on account of her speed. She achieved more than 18 knots on trials in 1957, and regained much of her youthful energy after being re-engined during the 1976-7 winter.

Oban, 'Gateway to the Isles', has always ranked as the busiest port serving the Hebrides. From the earliest days of photography the bay seemed to be filled with ships. This view, dating from *circa* 1976, shows the *Bute* (centre) heading for the spare Railway Pier berth ahead of the *Iona* (right, now with elongated exhausts). The *Bute*, one of three pioneering Clyde car ferries in the 1950s, was based intermittently at Oban and Mallaig between 1972 and 1978, the year of her withdrawal, after which she was sold to Greece. The ferry at the North Pier (left) is the *Caledonia*, built for the Stena Line of Gothenburg in 1966 and acquired by the Caledonian Steam Packet Company in 1970 to inaugurate its drive-through service from Ardrossan to Brodick, on which she proved a mixed blessing. She moved to the Oban-Craignure run in the summer of 1976, usually reverting to the Arran run in winter. Sold in 1988, she had a successful late career in the Bay of Naples, serving the island of Ischia under the name *Heidi*.

The *Eigg* was one of eight small bow-loading ferries, known as the 'Island' class, that came into service on shorter routes throughout the Clyde and Western Isles in the 1970s. They had space for up to six cars or one 25-ton lorry. In common with most of their larger successors, they were quickly found to be too small for the traffic. One of them started a new service across the Sound of Mull between Fishnish and Lochaline, another between Raasay and Skye, another between Gigha and Tayinloan on the Kintyre Peninsula. By the late 1970s the *Eigg* had settled down on the Oban-Lismore service. She is pictured (above) at Lismore in 2004 after her bridge was heightened, and arriving at Oban (right) with a cargo of cattle. 'Island' class ferries were still giving useful service after 40 years, though by 2010 only the *Eigg, Canna* and *Raasay* remained in the CalMac fold.

The *Pioneer* of 1974 revived a name with a distinguished history in the MacBrayne fleet. Purpose-built for the Islay service, with an open deck capable of carrying 30 cars or six articulated lorries and nine cars, she sailed from the old pier at the head of West Loch Tarbert until 1978, when CalMac took over the former Western Ferries' terminal at Kennacraig down the loch. Superseded by a bigger boat in 1979, the *Pioneer* served on a wide variety of other routes – a process known as 'cascading', whereby ships become victims of their own success on the run for which they were designed, and are assigned to lower-capacity services. The *Pioneer*, pictured on the Clyde in October 1998 while towing the *Loch Alainn*, was one of the fastest and most popular boats of the new generation of CalMac ferries. Sold to Equatorial Guinea in 2004, she left the Clyde with the name *Brenda Corlett*.

The *Claymore* was one of several general purpose car ferries built in the 1970s after the amalgamation of the Caledonian Steam Packet Company's Clyde services and David MacBrayne's West Highland operations. A novelty was the positioning of parallel funnels on either side of the hull, instead of the traditional single funnel amidships. But the *Claymore*'s most distinctive feature was the height of her superstructure, with a bridge four decks above her car deck. A product of Robb Caledon at Leith in 1978, she served initially on the Barra and Lochboisdale run, and later as the Islay boat. She is pictured on a rare visit to Lochaline (right). In 1997 she was sold to the Argyll and Antrim Steam Packet Company, a subsidiary of Sea Containers, to inaugurate a short-lived service from Campbeltown to Red Bay in Northern Ireland – though she was chartered back several times by CalMac, even appearing briefly on Clyde services. Thereafter she was acquired by Pentland Ferries, who had previously bought the *Iona*. Suffering from increasing neglect, she was sold in 2009 to a Danish company, which renamed her *Sia* and fitted her out as a cable-layer.

Built by Ailsa of Troon in 1979 for the Small Isles run from Mallaig, the fast and sturdy *Lochmor* belied her modest size. She had passenger accommodation on four decks and an arm-like derrick at the stern, capable of offloading anything from building materials to crates of soft drinks. She is pictured at Canna, an island she continued to serve until her replacement by the *Lochnevis* in 2000. After a brief sojourn at Campbeltown she was bought by a private operator in Devon, who remodelled her for day cruises on the River Dart, under the name *Torbay Belle*. She was later stationed at Poole.

The Modern Era

Caledonian MacBrayne has become as synonymous with Hebridean sea transport in the 21st century as David Hutcheson and David MacBrayne were in the 19th century. It sees itself as part of an evolving tradition of service – a tradition that began with a fleet of eight boats in 1851 and, even further back, with Henry Bell's pioneering journey by steamship into Highland waters. The landscapes, the waters and the calling points are the same today. CalMac red, slightly deeper than the old MacBrayne funnel colouring, is as distinctive a part of the territory as ever. But the scale of operations in the 21st century would be scarcely recognisable to previous generations.

The fleet, now wholly interchangeable between the Clyde and Western Isles, is owned by the British government under a complex corporate structure, devised in 2006, that separates legal ownership of piers and ships from employment of crews and day-to-day transportation. Its services are run as a monopoly, subsidised by and accountable to the British taxpayer. By the end of the first decade of the 21st century, government subsidy of CalMac services was approaching £100m – up from £26m in 2004 and £5.6m in 1990. The sharp rise in subsidy stems partly from the introduction of 'road equivalent tariff', reducing fares on some of the longer sea routes. It also reflects the taxpayer's commitment to an up-to-date service on unprofitable routes for the benefit of small island communities. In the year to 31st March 2010, the fleet carried 4.8 million passengers, 1.1m cars, 93,000 commercial vehicles and 11,360 coaches. It was the fourth consecutive year in which more than 4.5m passengers and 1m cars had been carried.

Today's services are maintained by 35 ferries (below, the *Isle of Mull*), several of them so large that on some winter crossings the crew outnumber the passengers. With comfortable accommodation and sophisticated navigational aids but often limited deck space, these utilitarian ships fail to inspire the affection their predecessors did. While the lure of the Hebrides remains the same (and who could resist CalMac's 'Hopscotch' deals offering extensive inter-island travel?), the islands are now marketed much like any other holiday destination. Their belated entry into the modern world may arouse regret among those wanting to keep the charm and beauty of the Hebrides a secret, but traffic numbers suggest more and more people want to discover them. Tourism has not only become crucial to the islands' economy, it has helped stem their depopulation. You are just as likely to hear English accents in the Hebrides today as Gaelic speakers; many incomers have bought properties and make their livelihood on the islands.

That the Hebrides can still be inhospitable is demonstrated every winter, when the seamanship of CalMac skippers is tested as much as their distinguished predecessors' was. In one such instance, on 11th November 2005, the freight carrier *Muirneag* spent 16 hours trying to enter Stornoway Harbour in a violent storm which had erupted while she was *en route* from Ullapool. Today's crews may have satellite wireless, powerful engines and bow thrusters at their disposal, but the ships they operate are several times larger than those of yesteryear, while often manoeuvring in the same narrow confines, such as Lochboisdale, Oban and Tarbert, Harris.

Having made do in the 1970s with a fleet dominated by second-hand ferries, conversions and Clyde cast-offs, CalMac in the 1980s began an extensive modernisation programme. Its most obvious manifestation was a stream of purpose-built tonnage, starting in 1984 with the *Isle of Arran* (below, at Kennacraig) and culminating with the construction of a new Islay ferry, the *Finlaggan*, at the Gdansk yard of Polish shipbuilder Remontowa, for entry into service in 2011. Equally important was the installation of link-spans at all remaining island piers where side-loading was still in operation. Meanwhile, the proliferation of ferry links in the Outer Hebrides made it possible to drive from Lewis in the north to Barra in the south.

Another change occurred on 19th July 2009 when CalMac broke the unofficial ban on Sunday sailings to Stornoway – in the teeth of opposition from Sabbatarian elements in the Lewis community. Lewis was the last bastion of Sabbath observance which, until the late 1960s, had been the norm throughout the Hebrides. CalMac's justification for change represented another step into the modern world: it invoked European Union legislation, which made it unlawful to refuse a service to the whole community because of the religious beliefs of part of it. EU legislation looms equally large in the stringent safety measures that must now be observed on all members of the UK's merchant fleet.

Admirers of an older generation of ships may bemoan the passing of simpler ways. They will have noted that the big CalMac ships no longer carry a Purser, the figure who once acted as a vital intermediary between company and travelling public: all tickets must now be purchased before boarding. And they doubtless regret that the modern design of Hebridean ferries reflects their prime function as vehicle and goods transporters rather than passenger carriers or models of elegance. But there have been benefits too – better timekeeping, greater comfort at sea, more ease of access to what, in MacBrayne timetables half a century ago, was advertised as Scotland's 'enchanted islands'. The enchantment is still there, and so is the escapism – as anyone knows who has watched from the deck of a ferry as the ropes are cast off from a mainland terminal and the bows are turned to the westward horizon.

With her spacious drive-through facilities and 76-car capacity, the *Isle of Arran* was the first CalMac ferry identifiably of the modern era – though her wooden railings and door frames offered reminders of an older tradition of shipbuilding. Launched late in 1983, the first of eight CalMac ferries built by Fergusons of Port Glasgow over a 23-year period, she entered service on the Ardrossan-Brodick run – initially with an all-black hull, though the white paint of the superstructure was later taken down to main deck level aft of the bridge. The *Isle of Arran*, nicknamed 'the Belgrano' by early crew members (after the Argentine warship sunk by the Royal Navy during the Falklands conflict), became a victim of her own success: traffic quickly built to the point where a larger Arran ferry had to be ordered. In 1993 the *Isle of Arran* moved to the Islay run, where she has spent most of her subsequent career. Among her many attractive features is the amount of open deck space forward and aft of the bridge. One of her few drawbacks is the lack of internal access from car deck to central accommodation block: passengers first have to brave the open deck. She is pictured at Castlebay, Barra, on 25th July 2002.

Since the 1970s CalMac ferries have regularly used Garvel Dry Dock, Greenock, for their winter refit. This view from February 2009 shows the *Isle of Arran* astern of the *Loch Fyne*, one of two open-decked, double-ended ferries built in 1991 for the Kyle-Kyleakin crossing. With accommodation for 36 cars and 250 passengers, the *Loch Fyne* and her sister the *Loch Dunvegan* had ample capacity for the Skye ferry, but after only four years they were made redundant by the new Skye bridge. Laid up in Greenock and put up for sale, both ships found a new lease of life in 1997 – replacing smaller CalMac vessels on the Fishnish-Lochaline run across the Sound of Mull, where the *Loch Fyne* has been an undoubted success, and the Colintraive-Rhubodach run in the Kyles of Bute on the Clyde.

The *Hebridean Isles*, pictured arriving at Colonsay in April 2002, was the first of CalMac's new big boats to be built outside Scotland – on the banks of the River Ouse in Selby, Yorkshire, in 1985. She took up the Uig triangle run the following year in succession to the 1964 *Hebrides*, inaugurating a drive-through service with her 70-car capacity – though a hydraulic lift and side-ramps were incorporated into her design for use at the shrinking number of piers where a link-span had not been fitted. Displaced in 2000 by the new *Hebrides*, the 'Heb Isles' has since worked on the Islay run, on which her upper deck observation lounge, allowing panoramic views on both sides and aft, is a notable plus.

The *Isle of Mull*, the Oban-Craignure ferry since 1988, was a shipbuilder's nightmare. As she floated off Fergusons' slip at Port Glasgow in December 1987, launched by Princess Alexandra with onlookers' cheers still in the air, sharp-eyed observers noticed she was too heavy in the water, meaning she would be unable to carry her contracted cargo weight. Fergusons implemented a series of weight-saving measures, but this was scratching the surface. CalMac needed the boat for the 1988 summer season and agreed to take her conditionally. The deal, reached before the ship was delivered, was that Fergusons would design a new middle section, with the job of constructing and inserting it going out to tender. Tees Dockyard, which won the contract for the 5.4 metre section, fitted it the following winter, with Fergusons footing the bill. Fergusons could claim credit for one by-product that was successfully incorporated into every subsequent big CalMac ferry: a children's play area, located on the extra deck space created by the new middle section. Although hardly a beauty, the *Isle of Mull* has shrugged off her early nickname, 'The Royal Barge'. Serving Mull and Colonsay from Oban, with occasional forays elsewhere, she has proved to be one of the most reliable members of the fleet.

The *Lord of the Isles* towers above yachts at Tobermory. After the axing of the Sound of Mull steamer in 1964, the island capital retained a direct link with Oban through the old Inner Islands mail run – the route for which the *Lord* was built in 1989, albeit divided into thrice-weekly sailings to Coll and Tiree and four-times-a-week to Barra and Lochboisdale. When a new *Clansman* came out in July 1998, the Tobermory call was dropped and the 'Loti', as she is known, was re-assigned to the Mallaig-Armadale summer service. Since 2003 she has performed a "mixed grill" of services out of Oban, sometimes sailing to seven islands within one week and even venturing into the Clyde in May 2004 to relieve on the Wemyss Bay-Rothesay run. She can carry 500 passengers and 56 cars.

The *Lord of the Isles* was one of the first CalMac vessels to have a bridge with full-length windows extended to the wings, rather than the traditional open wings exemplified by the *Isle of Arran* and *Hebridean Isles*. Not all skippers welcomed the enclosed wings: some like to 'sniff the air' while berthing. That led to the introduction of a sound reception system ('elephants' ears'), now mandatory, that allows the Master to listen to what is going on outside.

The mighty *Clansman*, built by Appledore Shipbuilders Ltd, North Devon, in 1998, was proof of the growing size and sophistication of the fleet. She and her sister ship, the *Hebrides*, command 5,200 horse-power from each of two German-built MAK engines, making them more powerful than the *Isle of Lewis* but not as fast, because of their higher 'block co-efficient' – the relationship between length, breadth and draught beneath the waterline. Powerful, useful and comfortable the *Clansman* and *Hebrides* may be, but they are no beauties. And, unlike their predecessors, they have a dearth of open deck-space, limiting opportunities for the travelling public to survey the magnificent Hebridean landscape. The *Clansman*, pictured (above) at Lochboisdale, operates CalMac's Oban-based services to Coll, Tiree, Barra and South Uist, and is the company's main winter relief vessel. The *Hebrides* sails on the triangle service linking Uig with Lochmaddy and Tarbert, Harris, where she is pictured (below).

With a service speed of 18 knots the *Isle of Lewis* is the fastest CalMac ship, crossing the Minch in two and three-quarter hours – about 45 minutes less than her predecessor on the Ullapool-Stornoway run. She is also one of the most capacious in the fleet, with room for 123 cars and 680 passengers. A product of Fergusons, Port Glasgow, she came into service in July 1995 and is pictured at the modern terminal which opened at the Lewis port on 14th May 1997. The *Isle of Lewis* operates a twice-daily service (thrice-daily on Wednesdays and Fridays in summer), and since 2009 has added a Sunday sailing, thereby breaking a centuries-long taboo on Lewis. In 2002 a dedicated freight vessel, the *Muirneag*, was introduced on a night-time service to reduce road hauliers' dependence on the *Isle of Lewis*'s daytime sailings.

No modern ferry in the Western Isles had a more tortuous start to life than the *Coruisk*, pictured leaving Mallaig with the *Lochnevis* berthed on the left and the *Waverley* in the distance. She was built by Appledore Shipbuilders Ltd, North Devon, in 2003, for the Armadale run in summer (where she replaced the popular *Pioneer*) and the Clyde in winter. No sooner had she entered service in the Sound of Sleat than she suffered a succession of technical problems, eventually running aground in Mallaig Harbour with the loss of one of her propellers. The widely reported incident gave her national notoriety. The cause of the problem was a novel form of propulsion – the double-propeller Schottel system, cheaper to buy and operate than the familiar Voith-Schneider units, but making the boat harder to control when manoeuvring at piers. The problem was eventually sorted, and the *Coruisk*'s plus-points – including excellent passenger accommodation – were finally appreciated. But her top-heavy, 'block of flats' appearance has won few admirers.

The *Lochnevis*, built at Ailsa, Troon, in 2000, is CalMac's Mallaig-based Small Isles boat, supplementing the service with twice-daily crossings to Armadale in winter. The *Lochnevis* is a hybrid ferry – boasting the speed, open-sea qualities and safety features of a larger boat, while also capable of berthing on a slipway like a small double-ended 'Loch' class ferry. She has a technical specification far beyond what one would expect of a ship of such limited capacity (14 cars, 190 passengers), and is the only triple-screw ship in the fleet (above). While on passage all three propulsion units are in use. At the slipway only two are used: power from the central unit is diverted to bow thrusters (housed in the gap behind the anchor chain pictured below), the engine thereby serving a dual function as propulsion unit and electric generator. When she entered service, some observers predicted that a ship with such a sizeable draught would have difficulty berthing stern-in at shallow slipways. It has not turned out that way: the *Lochnevis* has an extra-long stern ramp, and in the unlikely event of her touching down, her underwater protection bars at the stern safeguard the propellers.

RHOUMA

The *Lochnevis* lowers cargo onto the Eigg flit boat, *Laig Bay*, (inset) and awaits the return of the Rum flit boat, *Rhouma*, in Loch Scresort. The islands of Eigg, Muck and Rum were the last outposts of the time-honoured Hebridean practice of landing by intermediate ferry. In 2004 modern slipways were built to facilitate direct ship-to-shore transfer of passengers, cars and goods.

Some of the little 'Island' class ferries were superseded in 1986-7 by the double-ended 'Loch' class – four ferries with space for 12 cars squeezed between two narrow walls of superstructure. The 'Loch' class have, in turn, been superseded by larger boats, though some have 'cascaded' successfully to other services. The *Loch Linnhe*, pictured off Rhu Na Gal lighthouse on Mull (above), has become a familiar sight on the Tobermory-Kilchoan service, operating seven round trips per day, with five on Sundays in summer. The *Loch Ranza* (below) is equally useful on the service from Tayinloan to Gigha.

For many years the only way of getting across the Sound of Harris was by the Uig triangle service, usually necessitating two trips across the Minch. That changed in 1996: the 18-car *Loch Bhrusda*, a larger version of the 1980s 'Loch' class, inaugurated a new service between Leverburgh and Berneray, where she is pictured loading her three-lane car deck. Like other members of the 'Loch' class, the *Loch Bhrusda* is a double-ender: her skipper merely has to swivel his chair round to the other side of the bridge controls when the ship heads back on the return journey (overleaf). The *Loch Bhrusda* (pronounced 'Vroosda') is nevertheless unusual in having a water-jet propulsion system, judged to be less susceptible to damage in the shallow waters of the Sound of Harris than the flexible Voith-Schneider units that are standard in 'Loch' class ships. So successful was the *Loch Bhrusda* on the new service (doubling the number of cars carried in her first six years) that she was superseded in 2003 by a larger ferry and re-assigned to another new run across the Sound of Barra. For the first time it became possible to drive all the way from the Butt of Lewis in the north to Barra and Vatersay at the southern tip of the Outer Hebrides.

Bridge controls on the *Loch Bhrusda*

The *Loch Portain* took over the Sound of Harris run in 2003. Like the *Loch Bhrusda*, her predecessor, she was built at Bromborough on Merseyside, fitted with the same water-jet propulsion system and named after a local loch that had never previously been associated with a MacBrayne boat. She can take 32 cars and 195 passengers. She is pictured at Largs during a visit to the Clyde for overhaul.

The *Loch Buie*, built on the Forth in 1992, is a variant on the 'Loch' class. She has a recognisable bow and only one ramp (at the stern), and was designed for a run where vehicles are not usually carried – the crossing from Fionnphort to Iona, on which a ferry of the 'Island' class had been operating since 1976. The *Loch Buie* ties up overnight at a purpose-built berth in the Bull Hole, between Fionnphort and Kintra on Mull.

Like several others in the CalMac fleet, the *Isle of Cumbrae* was given a name to suit the locality she was designed to serve, only to find herself soon moved elsewhere. Built at Troon in 1976, she became a Western Isles 'steamer' in 1986, working on the Sound of Mull crossing between Fishnish and Lochaline, where she is pictured. After returning to the Clyde in 1997, she was assigned the Portavadie-Tarbert run across Loch Fyne. She has a capacity of 18 cars and 160 passengers.

The *Finlaggan*, the new Islay boat, is the first big CalMac ferry to have clamshell doors, and the first with a bulbous bow. Built by Remontowa of Gdansk, Poland (above, before launch), for entry into service in 2011, and regarded as a larger version of CalMac's two Rothesay ferries, the *Argyle* and *Bute*, she is the first CalMac boat to have had her name chosen by popular vote on the internet, Finlaggan being the historic site on Islay where the Lords of the Isles had their seat. More than 70 per cent of the 900 people who took part in the poll opted for *Finlaggan*, a name new to the fleet, in preference to traditional Islay steamer names such as *Pioneer* and *Lochiel*.

On 12th May 2002 the *Waverley* became the first paddle steamer to visit Coll (above) since the Second World War. Built in 1947 for the London and North Eastern Railway's Clyde services, the *Waverley* later passed into the ownership of the Caledonian Steam Packet Company and, in 1973, Caledonian MacBrayne. Sold later that year to the Paddle Steamer Preservation Society and now owned by a charitable trust, she is the only steam-powered vessel regularly undertaking public sailings around the British coast. Since 1981 she has rounded the Mull of Kintyre (below) to Oban (overleaf, top) for a short season of cruises in the Western Isles, calling at long disused piers such as Broadford, Crinan and Dunvegan, and in recent years venturing to a new pier at Inverie in Loch Nevis (overleaf, bottom). In two phases, between December 1999 and June 2003, the *Waverley* underwent a £7m restoration designed to keep her sailing for many years to come. She spends every July and August on the Clyde, and visits the Thames, the Solent and the Bristol Channel at the start and end of every summer.

Caledonian MacBrayne